Classroom-Ready

Number Talks

for 6th, 7th, and 8th Grade Teachers

Classroom-Ready

Number Talks
for 6th, 7th, and 8th Grade Teachers

1,000 Interactive Math Activities That Promote Conceptual Understanding and Computational Fluency

Nancy Hughes

ULYSSES PRESS

Published in the United States by:
Ulysses Press
P.O. Box 3440
Berkeley, CA 94703
www.ulyssespress.com

ISBN: 978-1-64604-012-4
Library of Congress Control Number: 2019951337

Printed in Canada by Marquis Book Printing
10 9 8 7 6 5 4 3 2 1

Acquisitions editor: Casie Vogel
Managing editor: Claire Chun
Editor: Renee Rutledge
Proofreader: Barbara Schultz
Front cover design: Justin Shirley
Cover art: © Ricardo Romero/shutterstock.com
Interior design: Jake Flaherty
Interior art: © shutterstock.com; page 11 © Designery; page 12 © Sandra Jones Illustration; page 13 © Michele Paccione

Contents

Decimal Strategies 111

Integer Strategies 130

Introduction

Purpose of Number Talks

Welcome to *Classroom Ready Number Talks*. This book was developed not to teach you how to do a number talk, but to provide you with a plethora of daily examples to use in your classrooms. Included are strategies along with number talks aligned to each specific strategy. According to Cathy Humphreys and Ruth Parker, authors of *Making Number Talks Matter*, and Sherry Parrish, author of *Number Talks: Helping Children Build Mental Math and Computation Strategies*, your students do not have to use every strategy, but it is important that they can use and understand at least one strategy, which will provide an entry point into a mathematical problem.

Although you can go through this book sequentially, its purpose is to find a strategy that will fulfill a necessary prerequisite prior to instruction. In this manner, you should be able to ascertain whether the student(s) have the necessary background knowledge to be successful or if they need remediation prior to instruction.

Please keep in mind, timed tests, drill and kill, and flash cards do not work if the student does not understand number relationships. Number talks create the ideal venue for teaching, reteaching, and reinforcing computational and reasoning strategies so students have the knowledge to solve many different types of math problems. This book is designed for any math classroom or program, including remediation, RTI (response to intervention), special education, general education, after school, summer support, or home schooling.

Number talks provide support for mental math and computational strategies. They are not intended to replace classroom instruction or to be used as a spiral review. The primary goal for a number talk is computational fluency (flexibility with computational methods, ability to explain their strategy, and computing with accuracy). Sharing math strategies during a number talk clarifies the students' thinking and helps develop the language of math. Through a number talk, students understand that numbers are made up of smaller numbers that can be composed and decomposed to make new numbers, making it easy to compute. Students have the opportunity to think first and self-correct if needed.

As you go through these number talks, you will see a heavy emphasis on the required fluency standards for each grade level as indicated by the Common Core Standards. Fluency means being fast but accurate, and number talks will help your students become lifelong learners of mathematics.

Required fluency standards as indicated by Common Core:

6.NS.B.2 Fluently divide multidigit numbers using the standard algorithm.

6.NS.B.3 Fluently add, subtract, multiply, and divide multidigit decimals using the standard algorithm for each operation.

7.NS.A.1 Apply and extend previous understandings of addition and subtraction to add and subtract rational numbers; represent addition and subtraction on a horizontal or vertical number line diagram.

7.NS.A.2 Apply and extend previous understandings of multiplication and division, and of fractions, to multiply and divide rational numbers.

7.EE.B.3 Solve multistep real-life and mathematical problems posed with positive and negative rational numbers in any form (whole numbers, fractions, and decimals), using tools strategically.

7.EE.B.4 Use variables to represent quantities in a real-world or mathematical problem, and construct simple equations and inequalities to solve problems by reasoning about the quantities.

The standards do not ask for speed and accuracy in computation but they do require the student to understand conceptually and work fluently with numbers so that students become proficient problem solvers. In order to be fluent and proficient with numbers, it is important for them to know and understand number relationships, and to be able to find entry points into a problem in multiple ways. Speed and accuracy will then follow. This can be accomplished through repeated practice in order to build automaticity, which makes a number talk a perfect daily routine.

There will always be students with unfinished learning, and number talks help these groups. Math is developmental, and it is essential that basic skills be practiced and reinforced daily. Number talks are a powerful way to empower students to become mathematical thinkers, efficient and accurate with computation and ready to problem solve. Traditionally, students used algorithms to solve math problems. Number talks help students see the relationship between numbers by discussing and sharing various computational strategies, so that when they use an algorithm, it makes mathematical sense and procedures become quick, efficient, and understandable.

Teaching, reviewing, and reinforcing reasoning strategies gives students the tools they need for lifelong learning.

Number Talks Focus on the Following Mathematical Practices

Number talks align quite well with the Eight Standards of Mathematical Practice. For example, during a number talk, students become engaged in making sense of the problem (Standard 1) while continually asking if their strategy and solution are correct or if there is a different or more efficient strategy that can be used. Through discussions, students are engaged in constructing viable arguments and listening to and critiquing the reasoning of other students (Standard 3). By listening and discussing, students look to understand the problem and find the most efficient way to represent and solve it. As a solution is determined, students focus on the precision of the answer and the strategy used to find the solution (Standard 6).

Standard 1: Make sense of problems and persevere in solving them. During a number talk, students look for strategies to find a solution. They consider the relationship of the numbers and plan a solution pathway.

If necessary during a number talk, help clarify a strategy. Number talks can help students find a strategy or pathway to a solution that makes sense to them. During a number talk, the discussing, analyzing, conjecturing, and discovering will help students understand mathematics.

Standard 3: Construct viable arguments and critique the reasoning of others. Students justify their solutions, communicate their results to others, and respond to the arguments of others.

A number talk can help students explore their thinking and conjectures. They allow students to make their arguments based on drawings, diagrams, charts, strategies, or manipulatives. A number talk can make math sing!

Standard 6: Attend to precision. During a number talk, students communicate precisely to others. They use clear reasoning strategies when sharing results.

By using a number talk, students communicate and use words and symbols of math to explain mathematical strategies. Students use their own words to calculate a correct answer mentally and explain how they did the math.

Standard 7: Look for and make use of structure. Number talks are all about looking for a pattern or structure by reasoning about numbers.

Number Talks in the Middle School Classroom

When should you use a number talk in the middle school classroom? Anytime during the school day; prior to math core instruction; or during morning work, whole group, small group, or intervention time.

How long will it take? Usually 5 to 10 minutes. It does not replace instruction.

What Does This Look Like?

+ Teacher presents a strategic computational problem.
+ Students are provided sufficient time to determine an answer mentally, giving a thumbs-up when they have an answer.
+ Teacher facilitates by recording student solutions.

- Student driven: Students share and explain their solutions as the teacher records their strategies.
- Teacher asks key questions to elicit discussion.
- Teacher is prepared to offer a strategy if needed.
- Class agrees on the correct solution.

Number Talks Purpose:

- Builds on prior mathematical knowledge.
- Helps students move from memorization of a standard algorithm to making sense of mathematics.
- Encourages students to verbalize their reasoning and explain their solutions.
- Teaches the importance of composing and decomposing a number.
- Strengthens both conceptual understanding and procedural knowledge.
- Provides 5 to 10 minutes to build fluent retrieval of basic arithmetic facts.
- Provides an ongoing practice with mental computation.
- Develops computational fluency.
- Provides explicit instruction on prerequisite skills.
- Models explicit strategies and multiple examples.
- Limits the number of new facts to two, plus one review.

Tips for a Number Talk:

- Number talks should be a daily routine.
- Mistakes are all part of the learning process. Use them as a teaching tool.
- Explore multiple strategies and multiple representations through a number talk.
- Keep number talks short; they should be about 5 to 10 minutes in duration.
- A number talk should not replace core instruction.
- Provide students with the time to explain their reasoning and thinking.

- Use problems you want students to master.

- When designing a number talk, think about basic skills your students need.

- Use problems in a number talk that a student will not only be successful with but will have multiple pathways to solve.

- Scribe student strategies so students can see the structure of their mathematical thinking.

- Have students explain why the strategy they selected works and makes sense.

- Remind students that they should not be using paper or pencils to solve these mental problems.

- Record student strategies for all students to see. Revoice (repeat back) a student strategy that was shared to make sure you and the students understand their method of solving the problem.

- Remember, just as the number line is important to addition and subtraction, an array and open array model is important for conceptually understanding multiplication and division.

- Start with small numbers!

- Post strategies and refer to them often.

As you share the strategies in this book with students, it is important for them to share their own strategies for finding a solution. Remind students to avoid the traditional algorithm when looking for a solution to each problem. Introduce strategies one at a time so as not to confuse or overwhelm. Keep in mind that a student only needs to find a strategy that makes sense to them and that will provide that entry point into a mathematical situation.

What Do You See?

Area and Perimeter 1

What do you see?

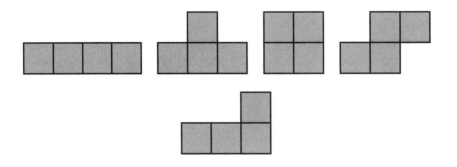

Number Talk Stems

- What is the area of each shape?

- What is the perimeter of each shape?

- How do the areas compare?

- How do the perimeters compare?

- Which shape has the largest perimeter?

- Which shape has the smallest perimeter?

- What do you notice about the shapes with the smallest and largest perimeter?

- Is there a pattern with the area? What is that pattern? Can you describe it?

- What conclusions can you make about the shape of the tiles and the perimeter?

- What are the dimensions of all the different shapes?

- How are all these dimensions related?

Area and Perimeter 2

What do you see?

Number Talk Stems

- What is the area of each shape?
- What is the perimeter of each shape?
- How do the areas compare?
- How do the perimeters compare?
- Which shape has the largest perimeter?
- Which shape has the smallest perimeter?
- What do you notice about the shapes with the smallest and largest perimeter?
- Is there a pattern with the area? What is that pattern? Can you describe it?

- What conclusions can you make about the shape of the tiles and the perimeter?
- What are the dimensions of each of the different shapes?
- How are all these dimensions related?
- How can you find the area of the next shape in the sequence? What strategy can you use?
- What is the area of the next shape in the sequence?

Volume

What do you see?

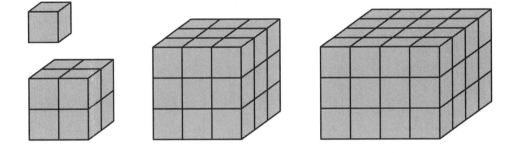

Number Talk Stems

- What is the area of each shape's face? Will each shape's face have the same area?

- What is the perimeter of each shape's face?

- How do the areas compare within the shape and with the other shapes?

- How do the perimeters compare with the other shapes?

- What is the volume of each shape?

- What is the surface area of each shape?

- Is there a pattern with the volume? What is that pattern? Can you describe it?

- What conclusions can you make about the shape of the cubes and their volume?

- What are the dimensions of all the different shapes?

- How are all these dimensions related?

- How can you find the volume of the next shape in the sequence? What strategy can you use?

- What is the volume of the next shape in the sequence?

Fair Shares 1

What do you see?

How can six people equally share four sandwiches?

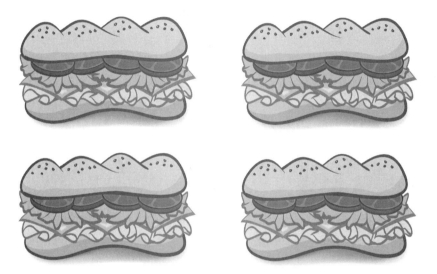

Number Talk Stems

- Do you have a strategy to solve this problem?

- Can you explain your strategy to a classmate?

- How did you find your answer?

- Did anyone use a different strategy they want to share?

- Which strategy makes the most sense to you?

- What operation will you use to solve this problem?

- Can you explain your thinking?

Fair Shares 2

What do you see?

How can three friends equally share four pies?

Number Talk Stems

- Do you have a strategy to solve this problem?

- Can you explain your strategy to a classmate?

- How did you find your answer?

- Did anyone use a different strategy they want to share?

- Which strategy makes the most sense to you?

- What operation will you use to solve this problem?

- Can you explain your thinking?

Fair Shares 3

What do you see?

How can three friends equally share five peanut butter sandwiches?

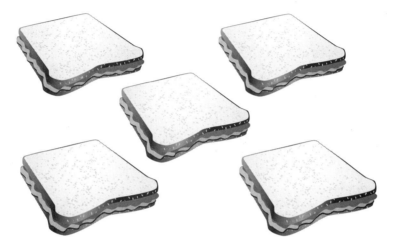

Number Talk Stems

- Do you have a strategy to solve this problem?

- Can you explain your strategy to a classmate?

- How did you find your answer?

- Did anyone use a different strategy they want to share?

- Which strategy makes the most sense to you?

- What operation will you use to solve this problem?

- Can you explain your thinking?

Partitioning 1

What do you see?

Which shapes are correctly partitioned in fourths? How do you know?

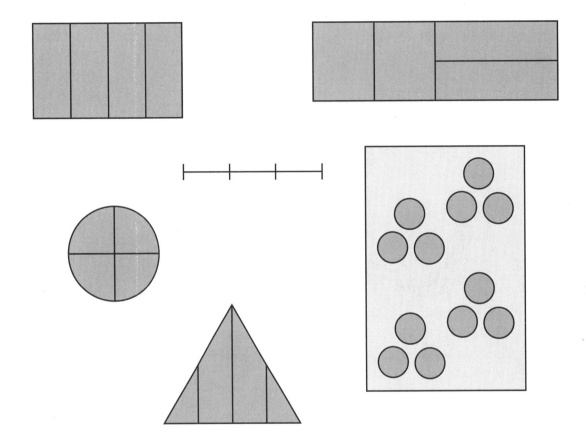

Number Talk Stems

- Do you have a strategy to solve this problem?

- Can you explain your strategy to a classmate?

- How did you find your answer?

- Did anyone use a different strategy they want to share?

- Which strategy makes the most sense to you?

- Can you explain your thinking?

Partitioning 2

What do you see?

What part of this whole is $\frac{2}{10}$?

Share your strategy.

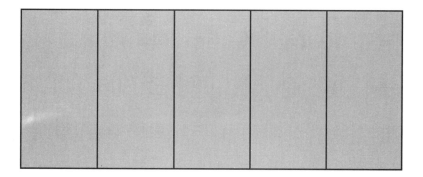

Number Talk Stems

- Do you have a strategy to solve this problem?

- Can you explain your strategy to a classmate?

- How did you find your answer?

- Did anyone use a different strategy they want to share?

- Which strategy makes the most sense to you?

- Can you explain your thinking?

Partitioning 3

What do you see?

How many fourths are in $\frac{5}{8}$?

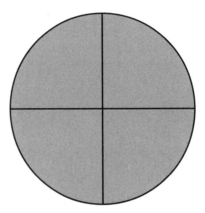

Number Talk Stems

- Do you have a strategy to solve this problem?

- Can you explain your strategy to a classmate?

- How did you find your answer?

- Did anyone use a different strategy they want to share?

- Which strategy makes the most sense to you?

- Can you explain your thinking?

Partitioning 4

What do you see?

What fraction is shown below?

Explain your strategy.

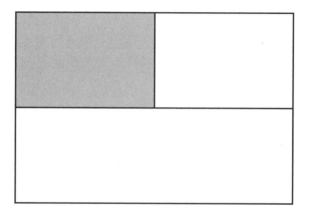

Number Talk Stems

- Do you have a strategy to solve this problem?

- Can you explain your strategy to a classmate?

- How did you find your answer?

- Did anyone use a different strategy they want to share?

- Which strategy makes the most sense to you?

- Can you explain your thinking?

Partitioning 5

What do you see?

What fraction is shown below?

Explain your strategy.

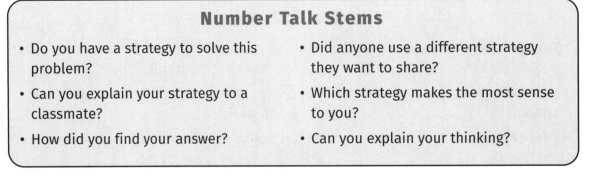

Number Talk Stems

- Do you have a strategy to solve this problem?

- Can you explain your strategy to a classmate?

- How did you find your answer?

- Did anyone use a different strategy they want to share?

- Which strategy makes the most sense to you?

- Can you explain your thinking?

Partitioning 6

What do you see?

What fraction is shown below?

Explain your strategy.

0   1

Partitioning 7

What do you see?

What fraction is shown below?

Explain your strategy.

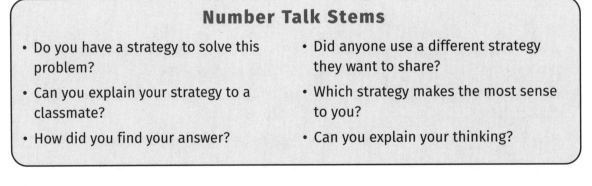

Number Talk Stems

- Do you have a strategy to solve this problem?

- Can you explain your strategy to a classmate?

- How did you find your answer?

- Did anyone use a different strategy they want to share?

- Which strategy makes the most sense to you?

- Can you explain your thinking?

Set Models 1

What do you see?

If 8 counters are a whole set, how many counters are in one-fourth of a set?

Explain your strategy.

Number Talk Stems

- Do you have a strategy to solve this problem?

- Can you explain your strategy to a classmate?

- How did you find your answer?

- Did anyone use a different strategy they want to share?

- Which strategy makes the most sense to you?

- Can you explain your thinking?

Set Models 2

What do you see?

If 15 counters are a whole set, how many counters are in three-fifths of a set?

Explain your strategy.

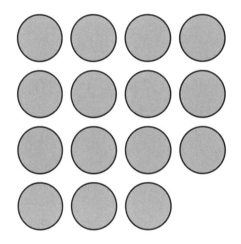

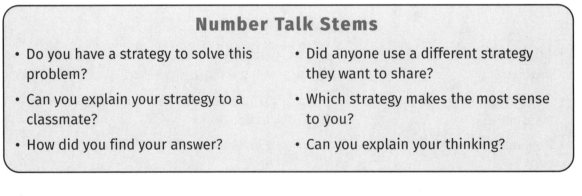

Number Talk Stems

- Do you have a strategy to solve this problem?

- Can you explain your strategy to a classmate?

- How did you find your answer?

- Did anyone use a different strategy they want to share?

- Which strategy makes the most sense to you?

- Can you explain your thinking?

Set Models 3

What do you see?

If 12 counters are three-fourths of a set, how many counters are in a full set?

Explain your strategy.

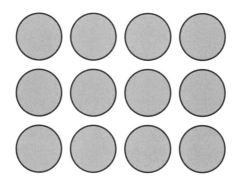

Number Talk Stems

- Do you have a strategy to solve this problem?

- Can you explain your strategy to a classmate?

- How did you find your answer?

- Did anyone use a different strategy they want to share?

- Which strategy makes the most sense to you?

- Can you explain your thinking?

Set Models 4

What do you see?

If 10 counters are five-halves of a set, how many counters are in one set?

Explain your strategy.

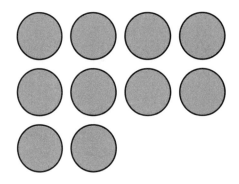

Number Talk Stems

- Do you have a strategy to solve this problem?

- Can you explain your strategy to a classmate?

- How did you find your answer?

- Did anyone use a different strategy they want to share?

- Which strategy makes the most sense to you?

- Can you explain your thinking?

More Than, Less Than, or Equal to One Whole 1?

What do you see?

Will the fractions shown below make a number that is greater than, less than, or equal to one whole?

Explain how you know.

Number Talk Stems

- Do you have a strategy to solve this problem?

- Can you explain your strategy to a classmate?

- How did you find your answer?

- Did anyone use a different strategy they want to share?

- Which strategy makes the most sense to you?

- Can you explain your thinking?

More Than, Less Than, or Equal to One Whole 2?

What do you see?

Will the fractions shown below make a number that is greater than, less than, or equal to one whole?

Explain how you know.

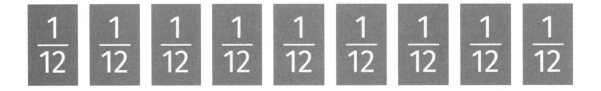

Number Talk Stems

- Do you have a strategy to solve this problem?

- Can you explain your strategy to a classmate?

- How did you find your answer?

- Did anyone use a different strategy they want to share?

- Which strategy makes the most sense to you?

- Can you explain your thinking?

More Than, Less Than, or Equal to One Whole 3?

What do you see?

Will the fractions shown below make a number that is greater than, less than, or equal to one whole?

Explain how you know.

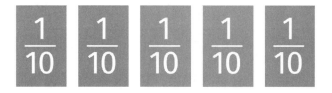

Number Talk Stems

- Do you have a strategy to solve this problem?

- Can you explain your strategy to a classmate?

- How did you find your answer?

- Did anyone use a different strategy they want to share?

- Which strategy makes the most sense to you?

- Can you explain your thinking?

More Than, Less Than, or Equal to One Whole 4?

What do you see?

Will the fractions shown below make a number that is greater than, less than, or equal to one whole?

Explain how you know.

Number Talk Stems

- Do you have a strategy to solve this problem?

- Can you explain your strategy to a classmate?

- How did you find your answer?

- Did anyone use a different strategy they want to share?

- Which strategy makes the most sense to you?

- Can you explain your thinking?

More Than, Less Than, or Equal to One Whole 5?

What do you see?

Will the fractions shown below make a number that is greater than, less than, or equal to one whole?

Explain how you know.

Number Talk Stems

- Do you have a strategy to solve this problem?

- Can you explain your strategy to a classmate?

- How did you find your answer?

- Did anyone use a different strategy they want to share?

- Which strategy makes the most sense to you?

- Can you explain your thinking?

Name That Fraction 1

What do you see?

Name a fraction that is closer to 1 than the following fraction,
but not greater than 1.

Number Talk Stems

- Do you have a strategy to solve this problem?

- Can you explain your strategy to a classmate?

- How did you find your answer?

- Did anyone use a different strategy they want to share?

- Which strategy makes the most sense to you?

- Can you explain your thinking?

Name That Fraction 2

What do you see?

Name a fraction that is closer to 0 than the following fraction, but not less than 0.

$$\frac{1}{10}$$

Number Talk Stems

- Do you have a strategy to solve this problem?

- Can you explain your strategy to a classmate?

- How did you find your answer?

- Did anyone use a different strategy they want to share?

- Which strategy makes the most sense to you?

- Can you explain your thinking?

Name That Fraction 3

What do you see?

Name a fraction that is closer to one-half than the following fraction,
but not greater than one-half.

$$\frac{3}{8}$$

Number Talk Stems

- Do you have a strategy to solve this problem?

- Can you explain your strategy to a classmate?

- How did you find your answer?

- Did anyone use a different strategy they want to share?

- Which strategy makes the most sense to you?

- Can you explain your thinking?

Addition Strategies

Adding to 100 or 1,000

What do you need to add to 48 to make 100?

> To make 100, I could add 2 to get to 50, then add another 50 to get to 100. Therefore, adding 50 + 2 to 48 would get me to 100.

What can you add to get to 100?

39	51	73
63	48	53

What can you do to get to 1,000?

245	645	785
498	568	881

Using the Distributive Property to Add

What is 15 + 36?

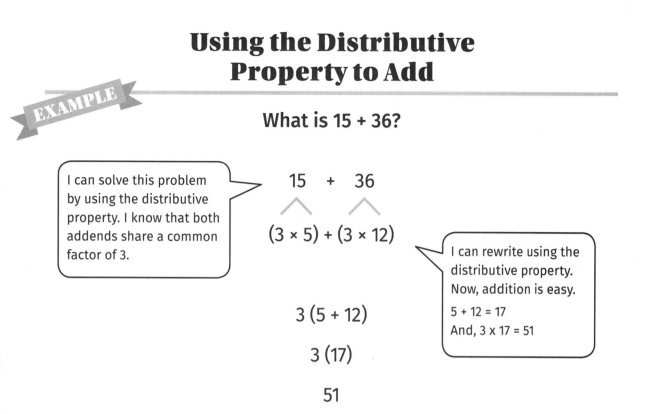

I can solve this problem by using the distributive property. I know that both addends share a common factor of 3.

15 + 36

(3 × 5) + (3 × 12)

I can rewrite using the distributive property. Now, addition is easy.

5 + 12 = 17
And, 3 x 17 = 51

3 (5 + 12)

3 (17)

51

What is...?

15 + 35	48 + 42	50 + 60
42 + 56	24 + 56	72 + 36
52 + 26	55 + 100	60 + 36
44 + 20	54 + 81	56 + 49

Adding 10

What is 36 + 29?

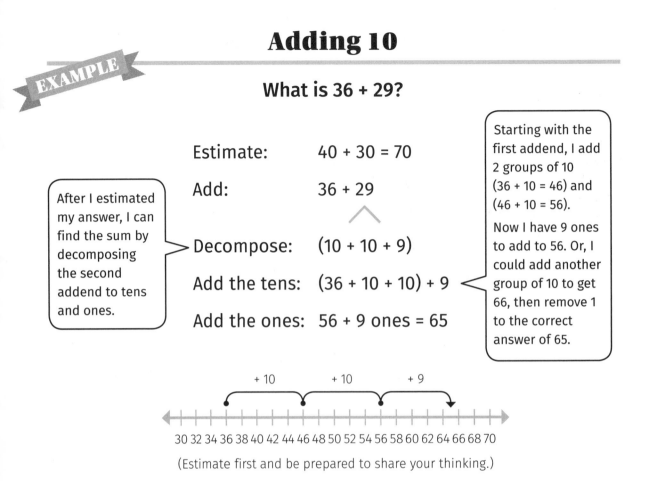

Estimate: 40 + 30 = 70

Add: 36 + 29

After I estimated my answer, I can find the sum by decomposing the second addend to tens and ones.

Decompose: (10 + 10 + 9)

Add the tens: (36 + 10 + 10) + 9

Add the ones: 56 + 9 ones = 65

Starting with the first addend, I add 2 groups of 10 (36 + 10 = 46) and (46 + 10 = 56).

Now I have 9 ones to add to 56. Or, I could add another group of 10 to get 66, then remove 1 to the correct answer of 65.

+ 10   + 10   + 9

30 32 34 36 38 40 42 44 46 48 50 52 54 56 58 60 62 64 66 68 70

(Estimate first and be prepared to share your thinking.)

What is...?

25 + 62	51 + 64	33 + 42
39 + 26	44 + 82	86 + 62
64 + 35	27 + 82	66 + 43
45 + 38	68 + 57	76 + 36

Decomposing to Add

What is 46 + 37?

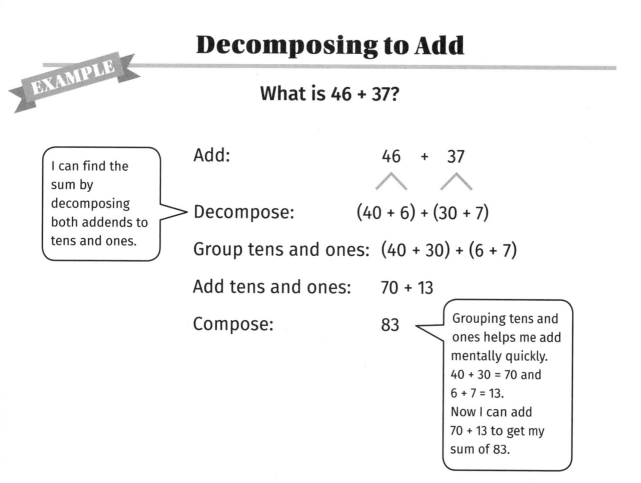

I can find the sum by decomposing both addends to tens and ones.

Add: 46 + 37

Decompose: (40 + 6) + (30 + 7)

Group tens and ones: (40 + 30) + (6 + 7)

Add tens and ones: 70 + 13

Compose: 83

Grouping tens and ones helps me add mentally quickly.
40 + 30 = 70 and
6 + 7 = 13.
Now I can add
70 + 13 to get my
sum of 83.

What is...?

51 + 54	29 + 72	48 + 58
82 + 91	83 + 25	112 + 67
314 + 98	34 + 122	321 + 52
173 + 112	95 + 89	152 + 143

Compensation

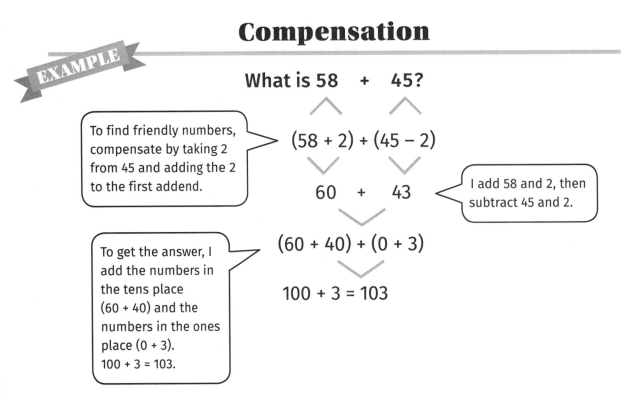

What is 58 + 45?

To find friendly numbers, compensate by taking 2 from 45 and adding the 2 to the first addend.

$(58 + 2) + (45 - 2)$

60 + 43

I add 58 and 2, then subtract 45 and 2.

To get the answer, I add the numbers in the tens place (60 + 40) and the numbers in the ones place (0 + 3).
100 + 3 = 103.

$(60 + 40) + (0 + 3)$

100 + 3 = 103

What is...?

59 + 26	85 + 49	98 + 34
32 + 48	119 + 84	77 + 58
76 + 38	137 + 47	126 + 94
49 + 53	186 + 45	115 + 27

Using Place Value

What is 154 + 163?

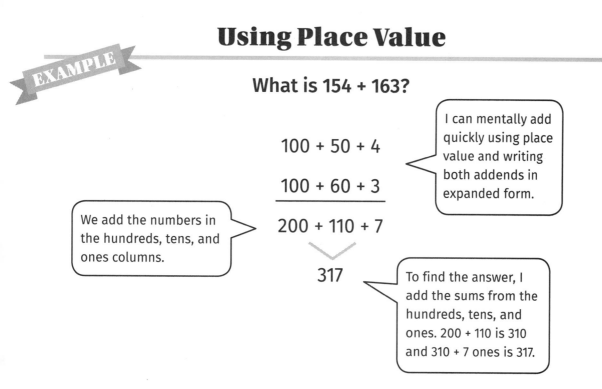

100 + 50 + 4

100 + 60 + 3
_____

200 + 110 + 7

317

I can mentally add quickly using place value and writing both addends in expanded form.

We add the numbers in the hundreds, tens, and ones columns.

To find the answer, I add the sums from the hundreds, tens, and ones. 200 + 110 is 310 and 310 + 7 ones is 317.

What is...?

88 + 94	121 + 324	126 + 79
237 + 721	434 + 176	228 + 112
132 + 435	341 + 344	659 + 183
586 + 382	197 + 338	259 + 841

Rounding Up

What is 134 + 289?

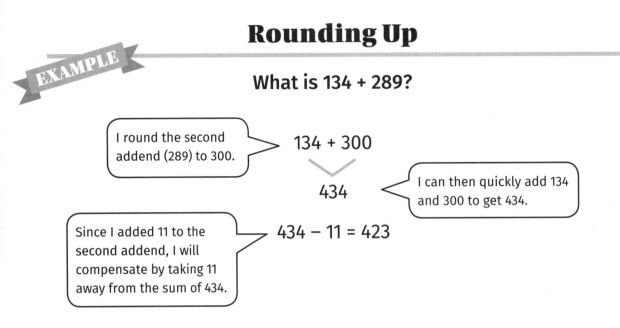

I round the second addend (289) to 300.

134 + 300

434

I can then quickly add 134 and 300 to get 434.

Since I added 11 to the second addend, I will compensate by taking 11 away from the sum of 434.

434 − 11 = 423

What is...?

345 + 295	118 + 88	389 + 168
156 + 179	521 + 191	199 + 199
467 + 292	287 + 194	249 + 179
398 + 198	119 + 296	313 + 151

Rounding Down

What is 457 + 209?

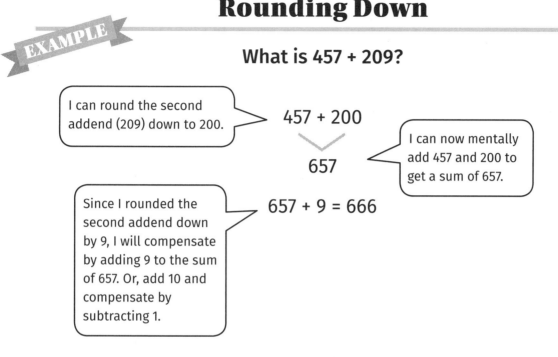

I can round the second addend (209) down to 200.

457 + 200

657

I can now mentally add 457 and 200 to get a sum of 657.

Since I rounded the second addend down by 9, I will compensate by adding 9 to the sum of 657. Or, add 10 and compensate by subtracting 1.

657 + 9 = 666

What is...?

435 + 201	589 + 509	394 + 402
459 + 112	484 + 108	696 + 313
287 + 321	292 + 204	495 + 306
119 + 102	697 + 205	897 + 313

Adding Left to Right

What is 1,256 + 3,423?

I begin by adding the numbers in the thousands place.

$$1,000 + 3,000 = 4,000$$

Next, I add the numbers in the hundreds place

$$200 + 400 = 600$$

Now I can add the numbers in the tens place

$$50 + 20 = 70$$

Finally, I can add the numbers in the ones place.

$$6 + 3 = 9$$

All that is left to do is add all the partial sums to get my answer for 1,256 + 3,423, which will be 4,679.

$$4,679$$

What is...?

564 + 235	6,346 + 1,453	2,456 + 1,133
236 + 742	4,412 + 3,586	6,254 + 5,142
912 + 384	3,636 + 8,213	5,678 + 4,321
686 + 414	3,451 + 6,327	3,456 + 3,423

Add Using Landmark Numbers

What is 788 + 456?

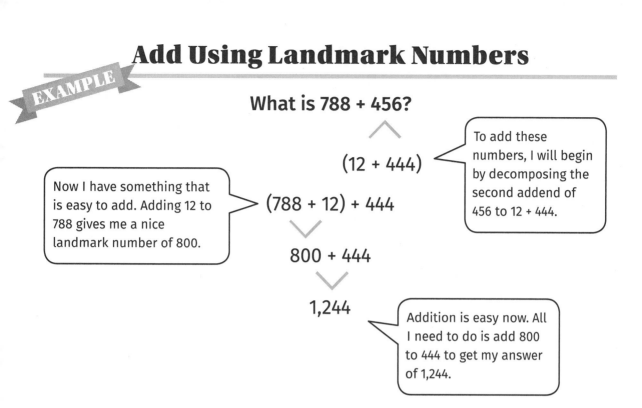

(12 + 444)

To add these numbers, I will begin by decomposing the second addend of 456 to 12 + 444.

(788 + 12) + 444

Now I have something that is easy to add. Adding 12 to 788 gives me a nice landmark number of 800.

800 + 444

1,244

Addition is easy now. All I need to do is add 800 to 444 to get my answer of 1,244.

What is...?

579 + 154	986 + 372	1,598 + 488
479 + 321	594 + 267	875 + 543
668 + 437	786 + 148	397 + 467
887 + 545	278 + 278	395 + 129

Jumping Up on an Open Number Line

What is 58 + 26?

I can use an open number line to help me add mentally. I begin at the first addend, 58, and jump by 20 to get to 78. My second addend is 26, which can be decomposed to 20 + 6.

I now need to jump 6 more units. So to make it easy for me, I jump by 2 units to get to 80 and then by another 4 (since 2 + 4 = 6) to get to 84.

My mental math strategy has me adding 20, 2, and 4 to get to the solution of 58 + 26, which is 84.

I could have started with either addend to find the solution.

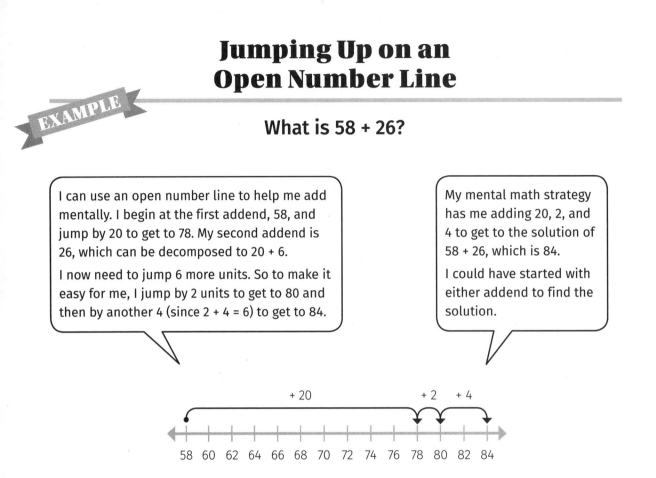

What is...?

92 + 36	89 + 23	34 + 23
118 + 45	124 + 54	68 + 36
84 + 29	58 + 49	44 + 38
68 + 43	84 + 37	76 + 34

Adding in Expanded Form on an Open Number Line

What is 3,456 + 2,123?

2,000 + 100 + 20 + 3

Addition is efficient when I add on an open number line. I start by writing the second addend in expanded form.

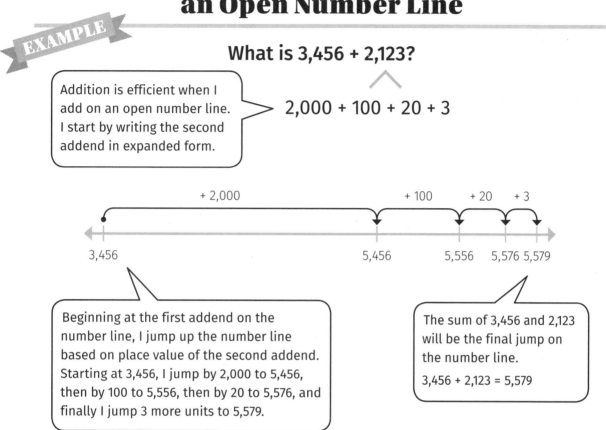

Beginning at the first addend on the number line, I jump up the number line based on place value of the second addend. Starting at 3,456, I jump by 2,000 to 5,456, then by 100 to 5,556, then by 20 to 5,576, and finally I jump 3 more units to 5,579.

The sum of 3,456 and 2,123 will be the final jump on the number line.

3,456 + 2,123 = 5,579

What is...?

4,567 + 2,345	7,123 + 2,873	7,124 + 6,234
3,256 + 5,587	6,789 + 2,185	7,235 + 5,645
1,235 + 3,356	3,456 + 4,456	4,345 + 6,864
4,567 + 1,236	2,546 + 2,643	3,457 + 2,128

Partial Sums

What is 56,335 + 32,456?

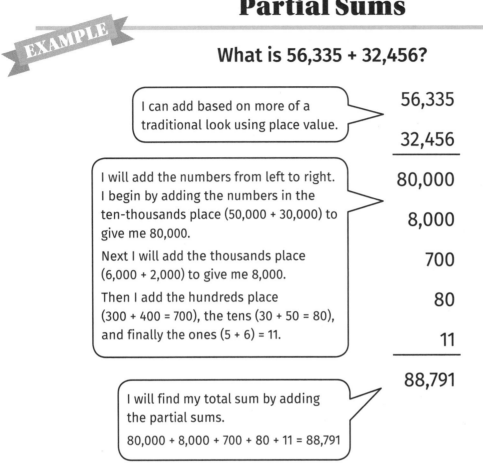

I can add based on more of a traditional look using place value.

56,335

32,456

I will add the numbers from left to right. I begin by adding the numbers in the ten-thousands place (50,000 + 30,000) to give me 80,000.

Next I will add the thousands place (6,000 + 2,000) to give me 8,000.

Then I add the hundreds place (300 + 400 = 700), the tens (30 + 50 = 80), and finally the ones (5 + 6) = 11.

80,000

8,000

700

80

11

88,791

I will find my total sum by adding the partial sums.

80,000 + 8,000 + 700 + 80 + 11 = 88,791

What is...?

34,562 + 21,574	34,671 + 14,431	34,631 + 52,541
15,235 + 42,435	45,253 + 21,547	45,641 + 16,341
13,264 + 34,121	16,234 + 42,641	56,834 + 93,384
34,585 + 12,231	82,109 + 45,346	31,785 + 83,735

Subtraction Strategies

Jumps of 10

What is 63 – 37?

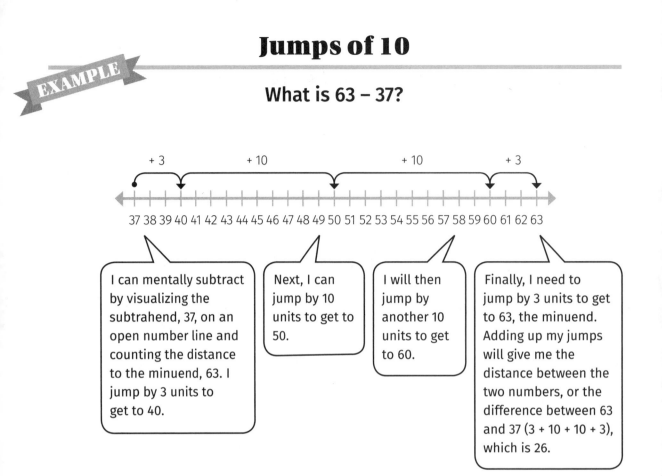

I can mentally subtract by visualizing the subtrahend, 37, on an open number line and counting the distance to the minuend, 63. I jump by 3 units to get to 40.

Next, I can jump by 10 units to get to 50.

I will then jump by another 10 units to get to 60.

Finally, I need to jump by 3 units to get to 63, the minuend. Adding up my jumps will give me the distance between the two numbers, or the difference between 63 and 37 (3 + 10 + 10 + 3), which is 26.

What is...?

59 – 38	96 – 68	82 – 29
114 – 96	212 – 98	105 – 53
118 – 49	94 – 37	82 – 58
74 – 48	154 – 94	174 – 118

Counting Down by 1,000s, 100s, 10s, 1s

EXAMPLE

What is 4,467 - 1,356?

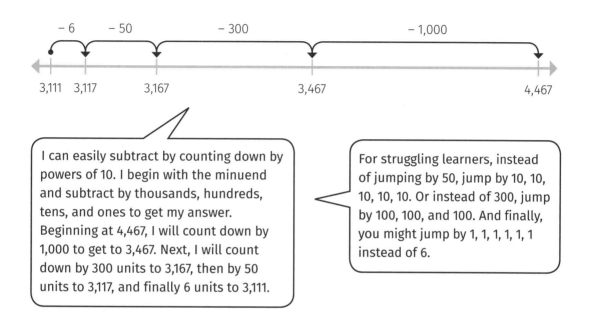

I can easily subtract by counting down by powers of 10. I begin with the minuend and subtract by thousands, hundreds, tens, and ones to get my answer. Beginning at 4,467, I will count down by 1,000 to get to 3,467. Next, I will count down by 300 units to 3,167, then by 50 units to 3,117, and finally 6 units to 3,111.

For struggling learners, instead of jumping by 50, jump by 10, 10, 10, 10, 10. Or instead of 300, jump by 100, 100, and 100. And finally, you might jump by 1, 1, 1, 1, 1, 1 instead of 6.

$$4,467 - 1,356 = 3,111$$

What is...?

5,236 − 2,124	9,458 − 5,235	8,976 − 5,642
8,458 − 4,326	9,678 − 5,552	7,968 − 5,745
7,898 − 5,547	5,797 − 1,654	1,495 − 384
3,567 − 2,335	7,895 − 5,004	7,884 − 3,671

Jumps Down by Groups of 10

EXAMPLE

What is 425 – 264?

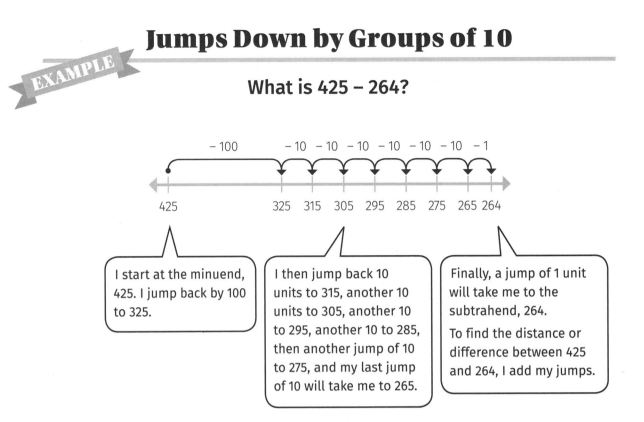

I start at the minuend, 425. I jump back by 100 to 325.

I then jump back 10 units to 315, another 10 units to 305, another 10 to 295, another 10 to 285, then another jump of 10 to 275, and my last jump of 10 will take me to 265.

Finally, a jump of 1 unit will take me to the subtrahend, 264.

To find the distance or difference between 425 and 264, I add my jumps.

100 + 10 + 10 + 10 + 10 + 10 + 10 + 1 = 161

425 – 264 = 161

What is...?

354 – 221	549 – 378	189 – 43
683 – 465	736 – 284	634 – 339
598 – 175	487 – 263	199 – 106
665 – 487	837 – 657	484 – 282

Decomposing

What is 78 - 42?

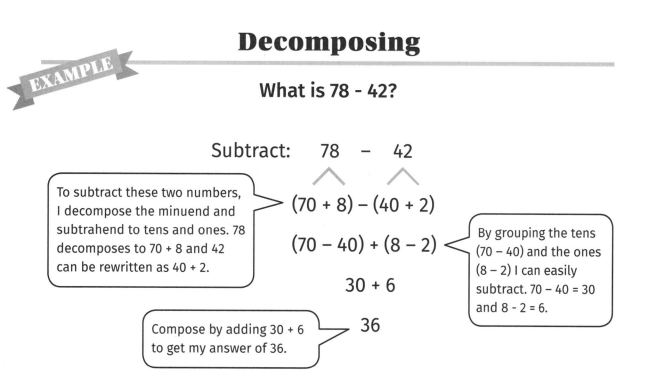

Subtract: 78 – 42

To subtract these two numbers, I decompose the minuend and subtrahend to tens and ones. 78 decomposes to 70 + 8 and 42 can be rewritten as 40 + 2.

$(70 + 8) - (40 + 2)$

$(70 - 40) + (8 - 2)$

By grouping the tens (70 – 40) and the ones (8 – 2) I can easily subtract. 70 – 40 = 30 and 8 - 2 = 6.

$30 + 6$

36

Compose by adding 30 + 6 to get my answer of 36.

What is...?

76 – 24	87 – 55	98 – 67
108 – 57	113 – 72	58 – 36
88 – 49	77 – 45	117 – 34
96 – 35	129 – 84	138 – 63

Compensation

What is 73 – 46?

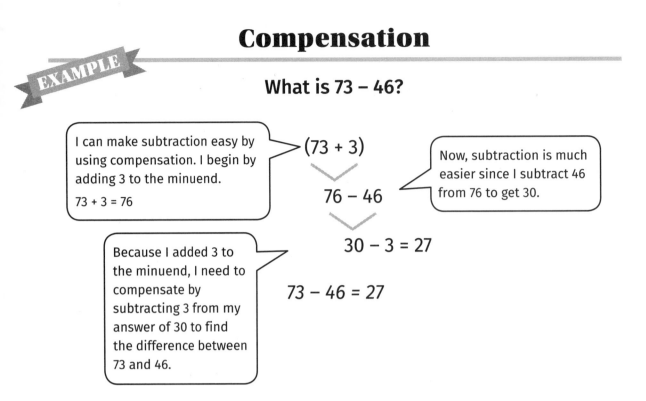

I can make subtraction easy by using compensation. I begin by adding 3 to the minuend.

73 + 3 = 76

(73 + 3)

76 – 46

Now, subtraction is much easier since I subtract 46 from 76 to get 30.

30 – 3 = 27

Because I added 3 to the minuend, I need to compensate by subtracting 3 from my answer of 30 to find the difference between 73 and 46.

73 – 46 = 27

What is...?

59 – 38	86 – 57	72 – 19
88 – 56	97 – 43	115 – 45
74 – 32	98 – 67	79 – 36
145 – 57	176 – 132	177 – 62

Subtract Using Place Value

What is 547 - 235?

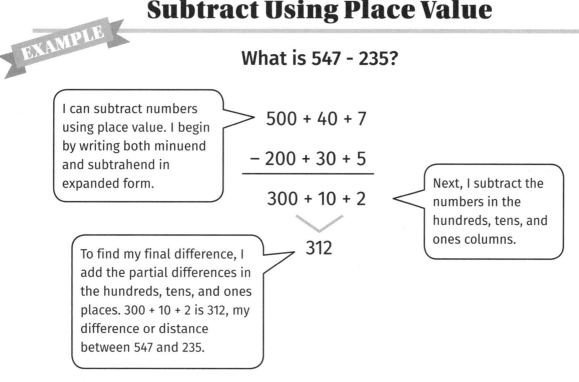

I can subtract numbers using place value. I begin by writing both minuend and subtrahend in expanded form.

$$500 + 40 + 7$$
$$- 200 + 30 + 5$$
$$300 + 10 + 2$$

$$312$$

Next, I subtract the numbers in the hundreds, tens, and ones columns.

To find my final difference, I add the partial differences in the hundreds, tens, and ones places. 300 + 10 + 2 is 312, my difference or distance between 547 and 235.

What is...?

681 – 345	598 – 195	327 – 112
467 – 332	319 – 216	789 – 325
787 – 335	1,298 – 973	2,376 – 842
969 – 431	879 – 543	3,393 – 1,271

Round and Compensate

What is 258 − 189?

To subtract these two numbers, I can round the subtrahend to 200. Now I have a set of numbers that are easy to subtract.

258 − 200

58

I subtract 200 from 258 to get a difference of 58.

11 + 58 = 69

Because I rounded 189 to 200 (189 + 11 = 200), I need to compensate by adding 11 to the difference of 58. 11 + 58 = 69. So, 258 − 189 has a difference of 69.

What is...?

459 − 199	132 − 75	364 − 181
658 − 281	243 − 96	452 − 294
700 − 395	195 − 84	521 − 379
900 − 788	1,000 − 575	800 − 699

Subtracting Using Expanded Form

What is 683 – 395?

I can subtract these two numbers by writing the subtrahend in expanded form, then using expanded form to subtract from the minuend.

300 + 90 + 5

I begin by subtracting the numbers in the hundreds place.
683 – 300 = 383

683 – 300 = 383

383 – 90 = 293

Next, I subtract the tens. (383 - 90 = 293) Or, subtract 80 to get to 303 (383 - 80 = 303), then 3 to get to 300 (303 – 3 = 300), then 7 more to get to 293.

293 – 5 = 288

683 – 395 = 288

Finally, I subtract the ones. Or, subtract 3 to get to 290, then 2 more to get your final answer of 288.
683 – 395 has a difference of 288.

What is...?

589 – 345	297 –186	872 – 126
897 – 456	399 – 286	973 – 453
393 – 118	196 – 102	879 – 372
573 – 264	934– 382	842 – 431

Same Distance on a Number line

What is 843 − 385?

Mental subtraction is easy when the numbers are easy to subtract. If I add 15 to both the subtrahend and minuend, I have numbers that can be easily subtracted.

$(843 + 15) - (385 + 15)$

$858 \quad - \quad 400 = 458$

Now we have numbers that are easier to subtract. 858 − 400 has a difference or distance of 458.

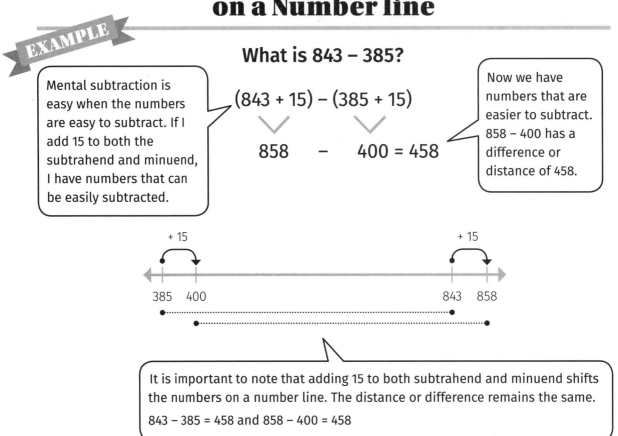

It is important to note that adding 15 to both subtrahend and minuend shifts the numbers on a number line. The distance or difference remains the same.

843 − 385 = 458 and 858 − 400 = 458

What is...?

891 − 288	191 − 85	791 − 588
768 − 189	393 − 195	829 − 455
765 − 199	459 − 181	304 − 195
543 − 281	598 − 293	505 − 275

Multiplication Strategies

Distribution Using Algebra Tiles

What is 145 × 4?

I can use algebra or base ten blocks to visually show multiplication. I begin by decomposing 145 into 100 + 40 + 5 using algebra tiles or base ten blocks as shown below. I place 100 (10 x 10) + 40 (4 tens) + 5 (ones) inside the T-bar with 4 and 100 + 40 + 5 on the outside of the T-bar.

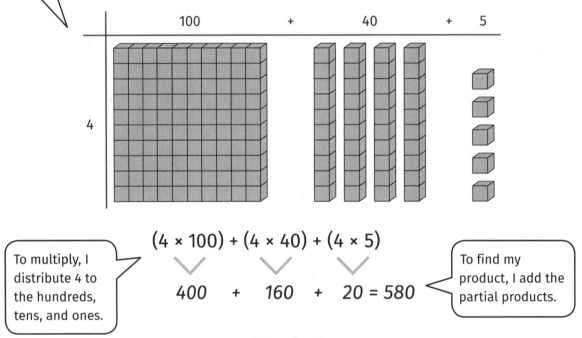

$(4 × 100) + (4 × 40) + (4 × 5)$

To multiply, I distribute 4 to the hundreds, tens, and ones.

$$400 + 160 + 20 = 580$$

To find my product, I add the partial products.

What is...?

158 × 7	282 × 8	153 × 6
321 × 5	635 × 3	847 × 4
117 × 9	234 × 7	1,213 × 5
922 × 6	576 × 4	683 × 3

Using an Array to Multiply

What is 23 × 5?

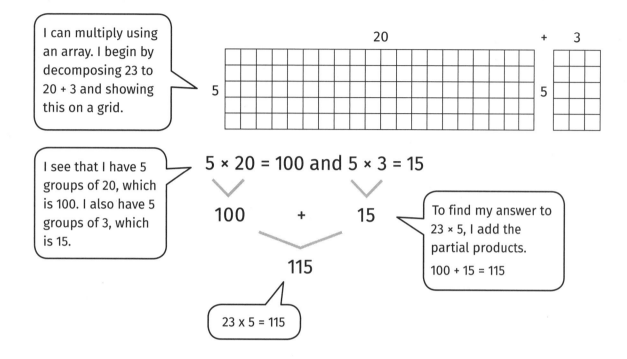

I can multiply using an array. I begin by decomposing 23 to 20 + 3 and showing this on a grid.

I see that I have 5 groups of 20, which is 100. I also have 5 groups of 3, which is 15.

5 × 20 = 100 and 5 × 3 = 15

100   +   15

To find my answer to 23 × 5, I add the partial products.

100 + 15 = 115

115

23 x 5 = 115

What is...?

64 × 6	45 × 8	23 × 11
36 × 12	28 × 13	86 × 5
28 × 7	32 × 8	45 × 4
81 × 3	68 × 7	23 × 5

Repeated Addition

What is 25 × 4?

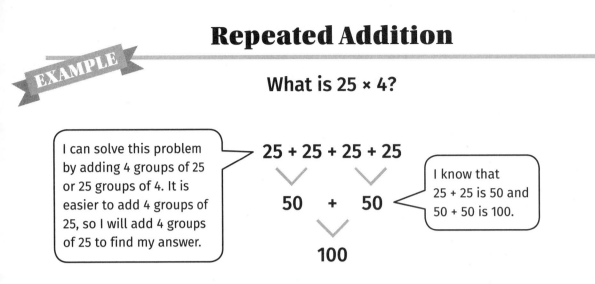

I can solve this problem by adding 4 groups of 25 or 25 groups of 4. It is easier to add 4 groups of 25, so I will add 4 groups of 25 to find my answer.

25 + 25 + 25 + 25

50   +   50

I know that 25 + 25 is 50 and 50 + 50 is 100.

100

I know that 25 x 4 is 100 using repeated addition.

What is...?

4 × 42	6 × 81	5 × 23
7 × 25	8 × 41	7 × 26
6 × 90	3 × 45	4 × 24
9 × 20	6 × 52	3 × 16

Known Facts

What is 6 × 12?

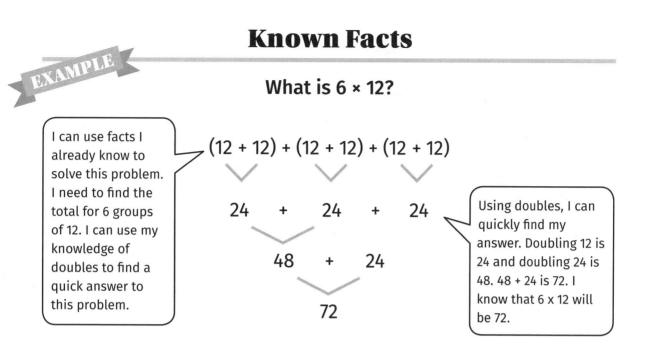

I can use facts I already know to solve this problem. I need to find the total for 6 groups of 12. I can use my knowledge of doubles to find a quick answer to this problem.

(12 + 12) + (12 + 12) + (12 + 12)

24 + 24 + 24

48 + 24

72

Using doubles, I can quickly find my answer. Doubling 12 is 24 and doubling 24 is 48. 48 + 24 is 72. I know that 6 x 12 will be 72.

What is...?

6 × 14	6 × 60	6 × 17
4 × 77	6 × 42	65 × 4
19 × 6	23 × 6	120 × 4
4 × 81	71 × 4	4 × 92

Round Up and Compensate

What is 24 × 18?

I can use mental math to quickly multiply these two numbers. I begin by rounding 18 to 20 and then compensate the 2 I added by subtracting 2 from 20. So, I change 18 to (20 − 2).

$$24 × (20 − 2)$$

Next, I decompose 20 to factors that are easy to multiply (10 + 10). Since the original number was 18, I will need to compensate by subtracting the product of 2 and 24.

$$24 × (10 + 10 − 2)$$

$$(24 × 10) + (24 × 10) − (24 × 2)$$

$$240 \quad + \quad 240 \quad − \quad 48$$

Finally, I add 240 + 240 to get 480, then subtract 48 or 40 and then 8 to get the final answer of 432.

$$480 − 40 − 8 = 432$$

What is...?

12 × 16	45 × 29	32 × 18
31 × 18	35 × 28	41 × 19
24 × 17	18 × 26	18 × 18
19 × 18	42 × 29	26 × 28

Round Down and Compensate

What is 32 × 24?

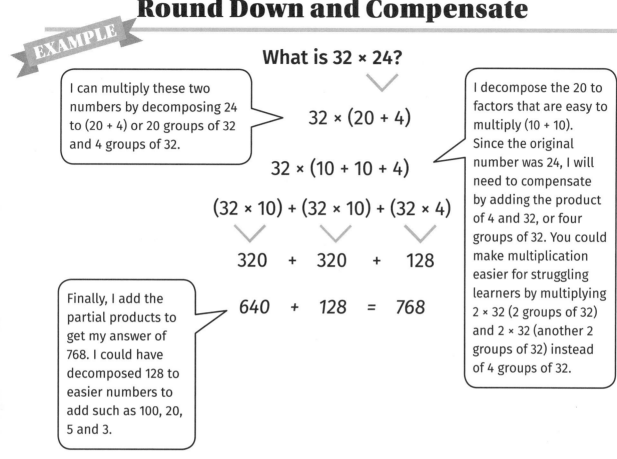

I can multiply these two numbers by decomposing 24 to (20 + 4) or 20 groups of 32 and 4 groups of 32.

$$32 × (20 + 4)$$

$$32 × (10 + 10 + 4)$$

$$(32 × 10) + (32 × 10) + (32 × 4)$$

$$320 \quad + \quad 320 \quad + \quad 128$$

$$640 \quad + \quad 128 \quad = \quad 768$$

I decompose the 20 to factors that are easy to multiply (10 + 10). Since the original number was 24, I will need to compensate by adding the product of 4 and 32, or four groups of 32. You could make multiplication easier for struggling learners by multiplying 2 × 32 (2 groups of 32) and 2 × 32 (another 2 groups of 32) instead of 4 groups of 32.

Finally, I add the partial products to get my answer of 768. I could have decomposed 128 to easier numbers to add such as 100, 20, 5 and 3.

What is...?

15 × 12	24 × 13	32 × 11
18 × 14	26 × 12	56 × 13
28 × 13	38 × 21	56 × 23
42 × 23	52 × 22	43 × 21

Multiplying Friendly Numbers

What is 9 × 24?

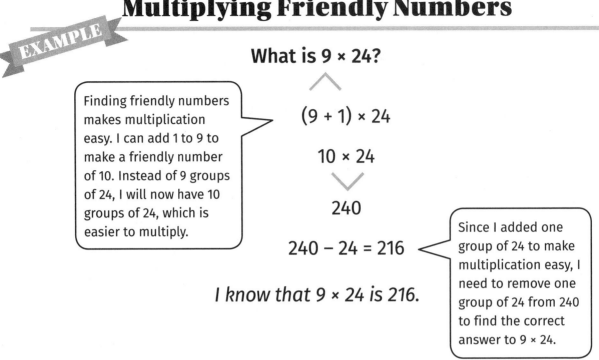

Finding friendly numbers makes multiplication easy. I can add 1 to 9 to make a friendly number of 10. Instead of 9 groups of 24, I will now have 10 groups of 24, which is easier to multiply.

(9 + 1) × 24

10 × 24

240

240 − 24 = 216

Since I added one group of 24 to make multiplication easy, I need to remove one group of 24 from 240 to find the correct answer to 9 × 24.

I know that 9 × 24 is 216.

What is...?

4 × 49	6 × 81	9 × 36
7 × 71	8 × 92	8 × 52
6 × 98	8 × 41	11 × 82
9 × 29	7 × 52	9 × 39

Doubling and Halving

What is 25 × 12?

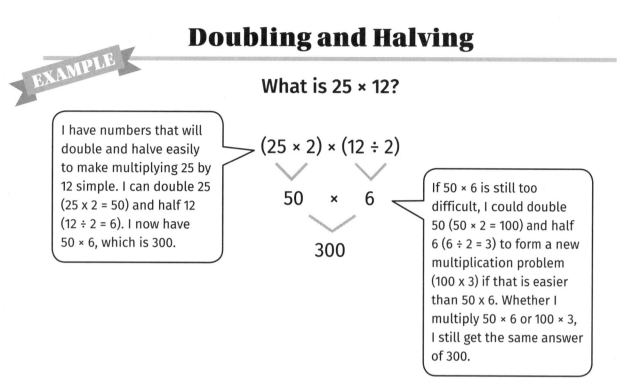

I have numbers that will double and halve easily to make multiplying 25 by 12 simple. I can double 25 (25 x 2 = 50) and half 12 (12 ÷ 2 = 6). I now have 50 × 6, which is 300.

(25 × 2) × (12 ÷ 2)

50 × 6

300

If 50 × 6 is still too difficult, I could double 50 (50 × 2 = 100) and half 6 (6 ÷ 2 = 3) to form a new multiplication problem (100 x 3) if that is easier than 50 x 6. Whether I multiply 50 × 6 or 100 × 3, I still get the same answer of 300.

What is...?

3 × 24	44 × 5	50 × 86
5 × 16	22 × 5	34 × 50
50 × 28	40 × 64	15 × 64
25 × 16	35 × 14	120 × 32

Distribution

What is 27 × 4?

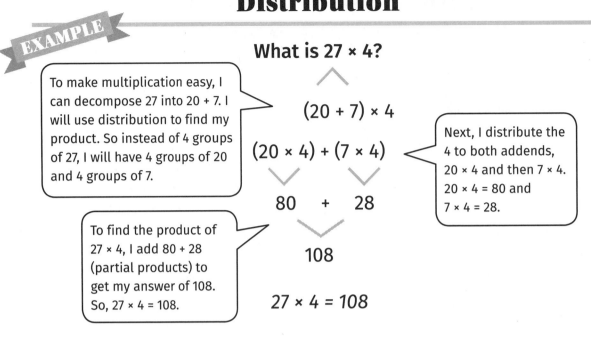

To make multiplication easy, I can decompose 27 into 20 + 7. I will use distribution to find my product. So instead of 4 groups of 27, I will have 4 groups of 20 and 4 groups of 7.

(20 + 7) × 4

(20 × 4) + (7 × 4)

Next, I distribute the 4 to both addends, 20 × 4 and then 7 × 4. 20 × 4 = 80 and 7 × 4 = 28.

80   +   28

To find the product of 27 × 4, I add 80 + 28 (partial products) to get my answer of 108. So, 27 × 4 = 108.

108

27 × 4 = 108

What is...?

58 × 5	82 × 7	48 × 9
126 × 3	75 × 6	92 × 4
38 × 7	448 × 4	96 × 9
47 × 8	76 × 7	48 × 11

Another Look at Distribution and Partial Products

What is 142 × 5?

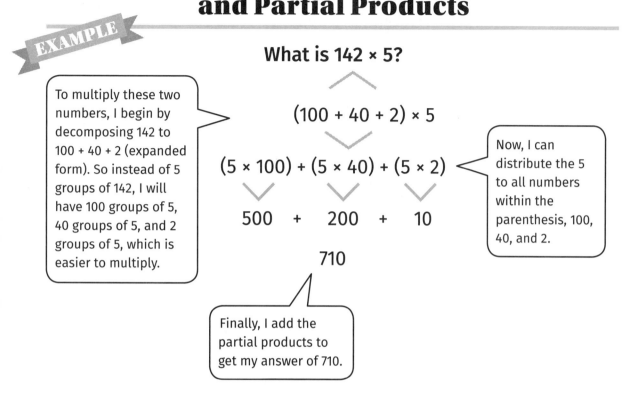

To multiply these two numbers, I begin by decomposing 142 to 100 + 40 + 2 (expanded form). So instead of 5 groups of 142, I will have 100 groups of 5, 40 groups of 5, and 2 groups of 5, which is easier to multiply.

$$(100 + 40 + 2) \times 5$$

$$(5 \times 100) + (5 \times 40) + (5 \times 2)$$

$$500 \quad + \quad 200 \quad + \quad 10$$

$$710$$

Now, I can distribute the 5 to all numbers within the parenthesis, 100, 40, and 2.

Finally, I add the partial products to get my answer of 710.

What is...?

36 × 9	84 × 7	56 × 12
93 × 6	25 × 14	18 × 41
46 × 12	94 × 22	34 × 25
31 × 34	52 × 11	72 × 23

Using the Associative Property

What is 25 × 12?

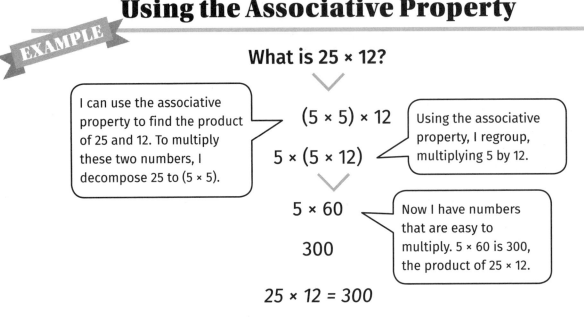

I can use the associative property to find the product of 25 and 12. To multiply these two numbers, I decompose 25 to (5 × 5).

(5 × 5) × 12

5 × (5 × 12)

Using the associative property, I regroup, multiplying 5 by 12.

5 × 60

300

Now I have numbers that are easy to multiply. 5 × 60 is 300, the product of 25 × 12.

25 × 12 = 300

What is...?

23 × 11	14 × 25	15 × 28
13 × 12	11 × 19	24 × 31
21 × 23	15 × 14	16 × 20
24 × 12	32 × 31	11 × 92

Using an Area Model

What is 27 × 43?

I can multiply 27 and 43 using an area model. I begin by decomposing 27 and 43 to tens and ones. I draw an area model, using (20 + 7) and (40 + 3) as the length and width of my rectangle.

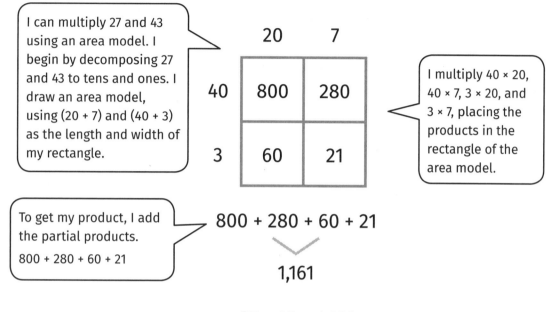

I multiply 40 × 20, 40 × 7, 3 × 20, and 3 × 7, placing the products in the rectangle of the area model.

To get my product, I add the partial products.

800 + 280 + 60 + 21

800 + 280 + 60 + 21

1,161

27 x 43 = 1,161

What is...?

34 × 45	26 × 32	42 × 24
86 × 52	97 × 12	76 × 57
47 × 36	49 × 64	84 × 63
81 × 57	76 × 82	59 × 72

Partial Products

What is 82 × 27?

Using more of a traditional approach to multiplication, I will multiply 82 and 27 and find my answer by adding partial products.

$$
\begin{array}{r}
82 \\
\times\ 27 \\
\hline
14 \\
560 \\
40 \\
1{,}600 \\
\hline
2{,}214
\end{array}
$$

Then I multiply 7 × 2 to get 14.

Multiply 7 × 80 to get 560.

Multiply 20 × 2 to get 40.

Multiply 20 × 80 to get 1,600.

Add partial products to find the answer.

What is...?

36 × 46	48 × 27	49 × 11
26 × 17	57 × 39	62 × 45
28 × 24	39 × 45	46 × 26
82 × 34	26 × 37	19 × 28

Division Strategies

Repeated Subtraction

What is 54 ÷ 9?

How many nines can be subtracted from 54? I can subtract 9 from 54 and keep subtracting 9 until I reach a difference of 0. Counting up all the nines that were subtracted, I see it took 6 nines to get to 0. Thus, there are exactly 6 nines in 54.

$$54 - 9 = 45$$

$$45 - 9 = 36$$

$$36 - 9 = 27$$

$$27 - 9 = 18$$

$$18 - 9 = 9$$

$$9 - 9 = 0$$

There are 6 nines in 54. Therefore, 54 ÷ 9 = 6.

What is...?

108 ÷ 6	750 ÷ 125	3030 ÷ 505
65 ÷ 5	1920 ÷ 320	280 ÷ 56
180 ÷ 12	1105 ÷ 221	620 ÷ 124
120 ÷ 30	267 ÷ 89	195 ÷ 65

Halving

What is 288 ÷ 24?

Mentally, I can divide quickly by halving the numbers until I find easy numbers to divide.

288 ÷ 24

I begin by halving both 288 and 24.

144 ÷ 12

Next, halve both 144 and 12.

72 ÷ 6

Now we have something easy to divide!

36 ÷ 3 = 12

36 ÷ 3

Finally, halve both 72 and 6.

12

288 ÷ 24 = 12

What is...?

96 ÷ 16	90 ÷ 18	52 ÷ 4
500 ÷ 25	70 ÷ 35	78 ÷ 6
184 ÷ 8	165 ÷ 7	144 ÷ 24
180 ÷ 36	72 ÷ 90	90 ÷ 15

Doubling

What is 105 ÷ 35?

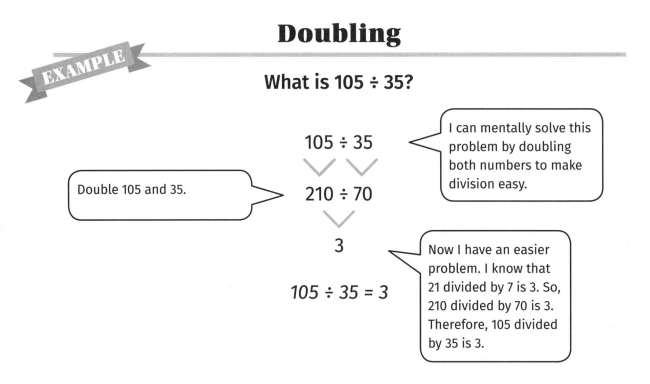

105 ÷ 35

I can mentally solve this problem by doubling both numbers to make division easy.

Double 105 and 35.

210 ÷ 70

3

Now I have an easier problem. I know that 21 divided by 7 is 3. So, 210 divided by 70 is 3. Therefore, 105 divided by 35 is 3.

105 ÷ 35 = 3

What is…?

120 ÷ 15	165 ÷ 15	325 ÷ 25
425 ÷ 25	245 ÷ 35	280 ÷ 35
135 ÷ 45	180 ÷ 15	360 ÷ 45
325 ÷ 25	180 ÷ 45	390 ÷ 15

Distributive Property

What is 624 ÷ 4?

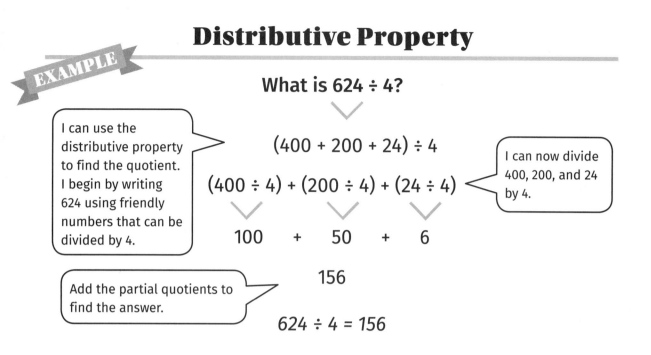

I can use the distributive property to find the quotient. I begin by writing 624 using friendly numbers that can be divided by 4.

$(400 + 200 + 24) ÷ 4$

$(400 ÷ 4) + (200 ÷ 4) + (24 ÷ 4)$

I can now divide 400, 200, and 24 by 4.

100   +   50   +   6

156

Add the partial quotients to find the answer.

$624 ÷ 4 = 156$

What is...?

232 ÷ 4	176 ÷ 8	606 ÷ 6
128 ÷ 4	273 ÷ 7	954 ÷ 9
525 ÷ 5	936 ÷ 3	960 ÷ 3
424 ÷ 4	847 ÷ 7	5,450 ÷ 5

Place Value Columns

What is 642 ÷ 6?

```
        1 │ 0 │ 7
   6 │ 6 │ 4 │ 2
       6 │   │ 42
       0 │   │ 42
```

This strategy has more of a traditional look. I start by looking at the 6 in the hundreds place. There are 100 groups of 6 in 600. 600 − 600 = 0.

Now look at the 4 in the tens place. There aren't enough groups of 6 in 40, so I move on to the ones place, adding the 40 to 2. We know that there are 7 groups of 6 in 42. Therefore, 642 divided by 6 is 107.

What is...?

600 ÷ 5	7,718 ÷ 2	249 ÷ 12
6,075 ÷ 5	847 ÷ 7	504 ÷ 24
396 ÷ 6	13,189 ÷ 2	972 ÷ 6
944 ÷ 8	576 ÷ 4	2,424 ÷ 8

Partial Quotient

What is 411 ÷ 32?

This is another strategy with a very traditional look. I begin by multiplying 32 by 1, 10, 100, 1,000, etc.

I know that 32 × 10 is 320 so I begin here. 32 × 1 would be too small and 32 × 100 would be too big. 411 − 320 = 91. I can't multiply by 10 but I can by 1. I continue in this fashion until I reach my remainder of 27.

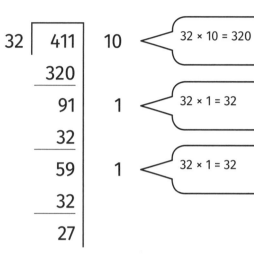

Multiply by powers of 10

32 × 1 = 32

32 × 10 = 320

32 × 100 = 3200

Add 10 + 1 + 1 = 12

Answer is 12 with a remainder of 27.

What is...?

432 ÷ 32	304 ÷ 19	268 ÷ 12
554 ÷ 23	150 ÷ 12	624 ÷ 68
496 ÷ 16	254 ÷ 24	556 ÷ 56
84 ÷ 21	168 ÷ 36	448 ÷ 52

Area Model

What is 375 ÷ 15?

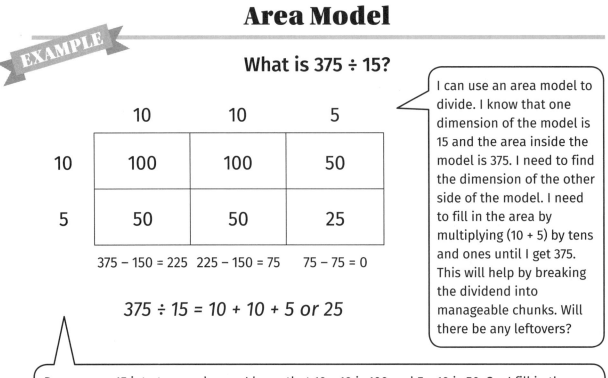

I can use an area model to divide. I know that one dimension of the model is 15 and the area inside the model is 375. I need to find the dimension of the other side of the model. I need to fill in the area by multiplying (10 + 5) by tens and ones until I get 375. This will help by breaking the dividend into manageable chunks. Will there be any leftovers?

$$375 ÷ 15 = 10 + 10 + 5 \text{ or } 25$$

Decompose 15 into tens and ones. I know that 10 × 10 is 100 and 5 x 10 is 50. So, I fill in the first column. Using repeated subtraction, 375 − 150 leaves me with 225. So, I multiply 10 × 10 and 5 × 10 again and fill in the second column. 225 − 150 leaves me with 75. 10 × 5 is 50 and 5 × 5 is 25. I can fill in the third column. Using repeated subtraction, I know that 75 − 75 leaves me with 0. Now my area within the rectangle is 375.

What is...?

128 ÷ 16	135 ÷ 15	324 ÷ 36
228 ÷ 12	504 ÷ 84	455 ÷ 91
221 ÷ 17	784 ÷ 7	168 ÷ 28
240 ÷ 16	156 ÷ 52	210 ÷ 15

Fraction Strategies

Comparing Fractions

Which fraction is greater, $\frac{5}{6}$ or $\frac{7}{8}$?

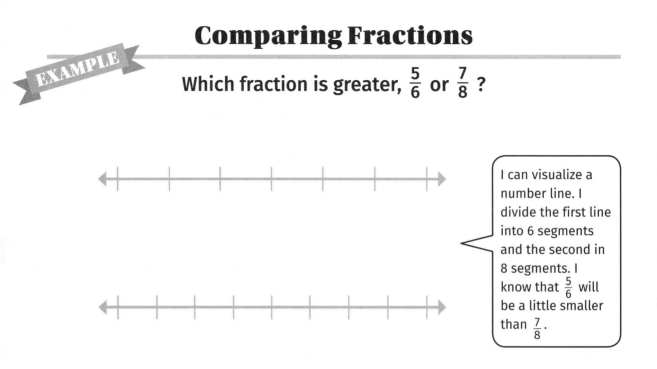

I can visualize a number line. I divide the first line into 6 segments and the second in 8 segments. I know that $\frac{5}{6}$ will be a little smaller than $\frac{7}{8}$.

What is...?

$\frac{5}{11}$ or $\frac{3}{4}$	$\frac{4}{10}$ or $\frac{3}{6}$	$\frac{5}{10}$ or $\frac{1}{2}$
$\frac{4}{5}$ or $\frac{4}{9}$	$\frac{3}{6}$ or $\frac{1}{12}$	$\frac{2}{3}$ or $\frac{3}{4}$
$\frac{1}{5}$ or $\frac{2}{8}$	$\frac{3}{4}$ or $\frac{1}{2}$	$\frac{3}{11}$ or $\frac{1}{4}$
$\frac{1}{2}$ or $\frac{3}{6}$	$\frac{5}{6}$ or $\frac{8}{12}$	$\frac{6}{12}$ or $\frac{12}{24}$

Decomposing Fractions

Rich decomposed $\frac{5}{8}$ into the fractions shown below.
Can you think of any other combinations?

I can think of several ways I can decompose $\frac{5}{8}$.

$$\frac{5}{8} = \frac{1}{8} + \frac{1}{8} + \frac{1}{8} + \frac{1}{8} + \frac{1}{8}$$

$$\frac{5}{8} = \frac{1}{8} + \frac{4}{8}$$

$$\frac{5}{8} = \frac{1}{8} + \frac{3}{8} + \frac{1}{8}$$

$$\frac{5}{8} = \frac{2}{8} + \frac{3}{8}$$

What is...?

$\frac{3}{4}$	$\frac{4}{6}$	$\frac{1}{2}$
$\frac{4}{12}$	$\frac{8}{10}$	$\frac{1}{4}$
$\frac{7}{8}$	$\frac{6}{12}$	$\frac{3}{9}$
$\frac{6}{9}$	$\frac{6}{8}$	$\frac{5}{8}$

Adding Using a Number Line

What is $\frac{2}{3}$ + $\frac{3}{4}$?

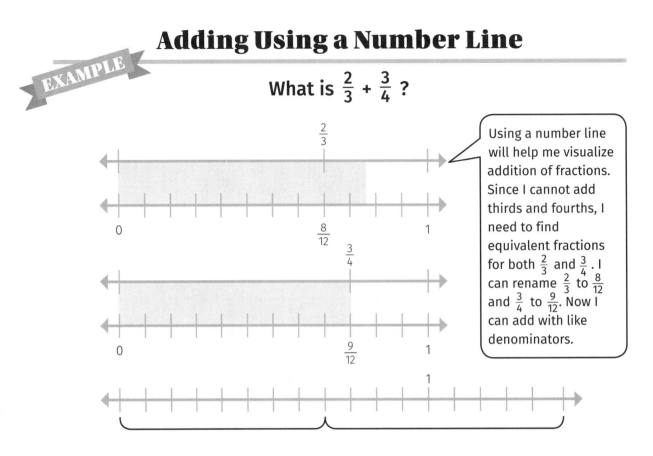

Using a number line will help me visualize addition of fractions. Since I cannot add thirds and fourths, I need to find equivalent fractions for both $\frac{2}{3}$ and $\frac{3}{4}$. I can rename $\frac{2}{3}$ to $\frac{8}{12}$ and $\frac{3}{4}$ to $\frac{9}{12}$. Now I can add with like denominators.

$$\frac{8}{12} + \frac{9}{12} = \frac{17}{12} \text{ or } 1\frac{5}{12}$$

What is...?

$\frac{3}{4}$ + $\frac{5}{8}$	$\frac{4}{10}$ + $\frac{3}{6}$	$\frac{5}{10}$ + $\frac{1}{2}$
$\frac{4}{6}$ + $\frac{4}{9}$	$\frac{3}{6}$ + $\frac{1}{12}$	$\frac{2}{3}$ + $\frac{3}{4}$
$\frac{1}{5}$ + $\frac{2}{8}$	$\frac{3}{4}$ + $\frac{1}{2}$	$\frac{3}{11}$ + $\frac{1}{4}$
$\frac{1}{2}$ + $\frac{3}{6}$	$\frac{5}{6}$ + $\frac{8}{12}$	$\frac{6}{12}$ + $\frac{12}{24}$

Adding Using an Area Model

What is $\frac{2}{3}$ + $\frac{3}{5}$?

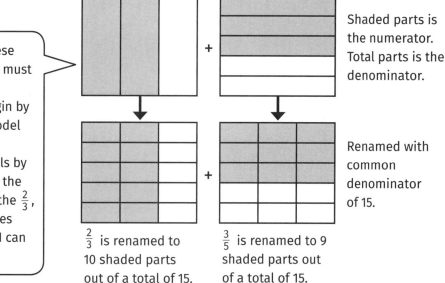

In order to add these two fractions, they must have the same denominator. I begin by making an area model of each fraction. I combine the models by placing the $\frac{2}{3}$ over the $\frac{3}{5}$ and the $\frac{3}{5}$ over the $\frac{2}{3}$, dividing both shapes into 15 parts. Now I can add.

Shaded parts is the numerator. Total parts is the denominator.

Renamed with common denominator of 15.

$\frac{2}{3}$ is renamed to 10 shaded parts out of a total of 15.

$\frac{3}{5}$ is renamed to 9 shaded parts out of a total of 15.

$$\frac{10}{15} + \frac{9}{15} = \frac{19}{15} \text{ or } 1\frac{4}{15}$$

What is...?

$\frac{3}{4}$ + $\frac{2}{3}$	$\frac{2}{6}$ + $\frac{1}{5}$	$\frac{1}{2}$ + $\frac{3}{5}$
$\frac{4}{7}$ + $\frac{1}{2}$	$\frac{4}{5}$ + $\frac{1}{2}$	$\frac{1}{5}$ + $\frac{5}{6}$
$\frac{2}{3}$ + $\frac{2}{5}$	$\frac{3}{5}$ + $\frac{1}{4}$	$\frac{1}{7}$ + $\frac{2}{6}$
$\frac{2}{5}$ + $\frac{1}{3}$	$\frac{3}{4}$ + $\frac{1}{5}$	$\frac{2}{3}$ + $\frac{3}{5}$

Decomposition to Unit Fractions

What is $\frac{3}{4} + \frac{7}{8}$?

$$\frac{3}{4} \quad + \quad \boxed{\frac{7}{8}}$$

$$\frac{1}{4} + \frac{1}{4} + \frac{1}{4} = \boxed{\frac{1}{8}} + \frac{1}{8} + \frac{1}{8} + \frac{1}{8} + \frac{1}{8} + \frac{1}{8}$$

> I can add by decomposing the fractions to unit fractions. I begin by decomposing three-fourths to 3 one-fourths and decompose each one-fourth to eights, making 6 one-eighths.

$$\left(\frac{5}{8} + \frac{1}{8} \right) + \frac{7}{8} = \frac{5}{8} + \left(\frac{1}{8} + \frac{7}{8} \right) = 1\frac{5}{8}$$

> Next, I combine 5 of the one-eighths to $\frac{5}{8}$ with a remaining $\frac{1}{8}$. Now you can combine $\frac{1}{8}$ with $\frac{7}{8}$ to make one whole with $\frac{5}{8}$ remaining.

What is...?

$\frac{5}{8} + \frac{1}{16}$	$\frac{3}{4} + \frac{3}{8}$	$\frac{1}{4} + \frac{5}{12}$
$\frac{3}{9} + \frac{2}{3}$	$\frac{5}{7} + \frac{5}{14}$	$\frac{7}{16} + \frac{3}{4}$
$\frac{2}{5} + \frac{3}{10}$	$\frac{4}{9} + \frac{2}{3}$	$\frac{2}{12} + \frac{2}{4}$
$\frac{1}{6} + \frac{5}{12}$	$\frac{2}{5} + \frac{3}{15}$	$\frac{5}{6} + \frac{2}{3}$

Friendly Fractions

What is $\frac{5}{6} + \frac{1}{2}$?

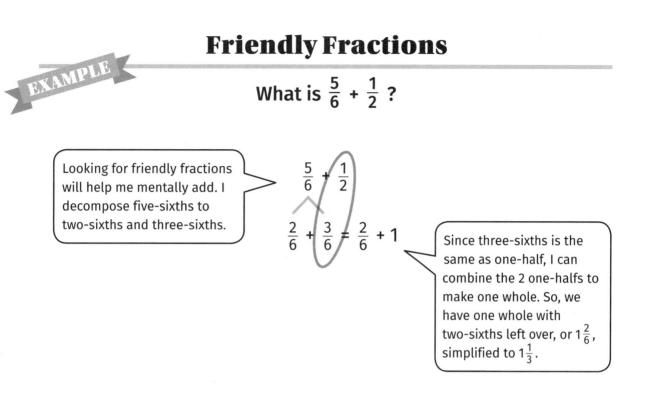

Looking for friendly fractions will help me mentally add. I decompose five-sixths to two-sixths and three-sixths.

$\frac{5}{6} + \frac{1}{2}$

$\frac{2}{6} + \frac{3}{6} = \frac{2}{6} + 1$

Since three-sixths is the same as one-half, I can combine the 2 one-halfs to make one whole. So, we have one whole with two-sixths left over, or $1\frac{2}{6}$, simplified to $1\frac{1}{3}$.

What is...?

$\frac{2}{8} + \frac{5}{16}$	$\frac{1}{4} + \frac{5}{8}$	$\frac{3}{4} + \frac{7}{12}$
$\frac{5}{9} + \frac{2}{3}$	$\frac{3}{7} + \frac{2}{14}$	$\frac{8}{16} + \frac{3}{4}$
$\frac{3}{5} + \frac{7}{10}$	$\frac{5}{9} + \frac{2}{3}$	$\frac{7}{12} + \frac{2}{4}$
$\frac{4}{6} + \frac{3}{12}$	$\frac{1}{5} + \frac{4}{15}$	$\frac{3}{6} + \frac{2}{3}$

Equivalent Fractions

What is $\frac{2}{3} + \frac{1}{8}$?

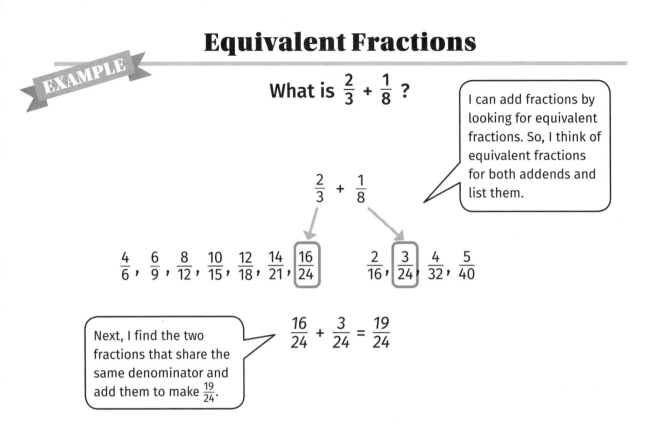

I can add fractions by looking for equivalent fractions. So, I think of equivalent fractions for both addends and list them.

$$\frac{2}{3} + \frac{1}{8}$$

$$\frac{4}{6}, \frac{6}{9}, \frac{8}{12}, \frac{10}{15}, \frac{12}{18}, \frac{14}{21}, \boxed{\frac{16}{24}} \qquad \frac{2}{16}, \boxed{\frac{3}{24}}, \frac{4}{32}, \frac{5}{40}$$

Next, I find the two fractions that share the same denominator and add them to make $\frac{19}{24}$.

$$\frac{16}{24} + \frac{3}{24} = \frac{19}{24}$$

What is...?

$\frac{3}{4} + \frac{1}{5}$	$\frac{2}{4} + \frac{5}{8}$	$\frac{2}{5} + \frac{1}{4}$
$\frac{2}{7} + \frac{3}{4}$	$\frac{2}{5} + \frac{2}{7}$	$\frac{3}{7} + \frac{1}{5}$
$\frac{2}{9} + \frac{1}{3}$	$\frac{1}{12} + \frac{4}{6}$	$\frac{2}{9} + \frac{5}{6}$
$\frac{2}{5} + \frac{3}{6}$	$\frac{1}{6} + \frac{3}{8}$	$\frac{1}{5} + \frac{3}{8}$

Fraction Tiles and Unlike Denominators

What is $\frac{7}{10} - \frac{3}{5}$?

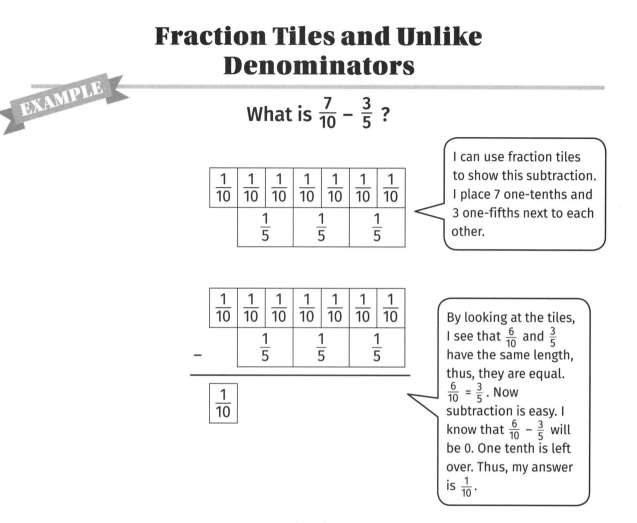

I can use fraction tiles to show this subtraction. I place 7 one-tenths and 3 one-fifths next to each other.

By looking at the tiles, I see that $\frac{6}{10}$ and $\frac{3}{5}$ have the same length, thus, they are equal. $\frac{6}{10} = \frac{3}{5}$. Now subtraction is easy. I know that $\frac{6}{10} - \frac{3}{5}$ will be 0. One tenth is left over. Thus, my answer is $\frac{1}{10}$.

What is...?

$\frac{3}{4} - \frac{2}{8}$	$\frac{2}{5} - \frac{1}{10}$	$\frac{9}{12} - \frac{2}{6}$
$\frac{4}{5} - \frac{4}{10}$	$\frac{5}{8} - \frac{1}{4}$	$\frac{7}{12} - \frac{1}{6}$
$\frac{9}{10} - \frac{1}{2}$	$\frac{3}{4} - \frac{1}{2}$	$\frac{9}{10} - \frac{3}{5}$
$\frac{5}{6} - \frac{2}{3}$	$\frac{9}{12} - \frac{1}{6}$	$\frac{4}{5} - \frac{3}{10}$

Subtracting Using a Number Line

EXAMPLE

What is $\frac{3}{4} - \frac{2}{3}$?

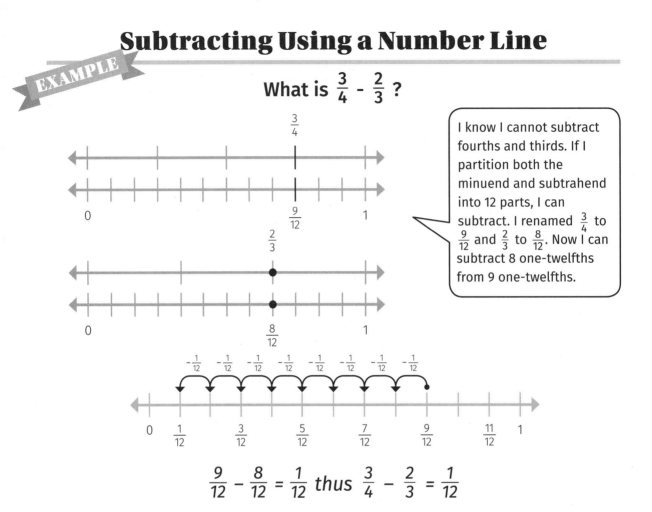

> I know I cannot subtract fourths and thirds. If I partition both the minuend and subtrahend into 12 parts, I can subtract. I renamed $\frac{3}{4}$ to $\frac{9}{12}$ and $\frac{2}{3}$ to $\frac{8}{12}$. Now I can subtract 8 one-twelfths from 9 one-twelfths.

$$\frac{9}{12} - \frac{8}{12} = \frac{1}{12} \ thus \ \frac{3}{4} - \frac{2}{3} = \frac{1}{12}$$

What is...?

$\frac{7}{9} - \frac{2}{3}$	$\frac{6}{8} - \frac{2}{4}$	$\frac{8}{12} - \frac{3}{6}$
$\frac{8}{10} - \frac{3}{5}$	$\frac{5}{8} - \frac{1}{4}$	$\frac{8}{12} - \frac{3}{6}$
$\frac{4}{6} - \frac{1}{3}$	$\frac{3}{4} - \frac{1}{2}$	$\frac{7}{10} - \frac{2}{5}$
$\frac{10}{12} - \frac{2}{4}$	$\frac{9}{12} - \frac{2}{6}$	$\frac{3}{5} - \frac{2}{10}$

Subtracting Using an Area Model

EXAMPLE

What is $\frac{5}{6} - \frac{2}{3}$?

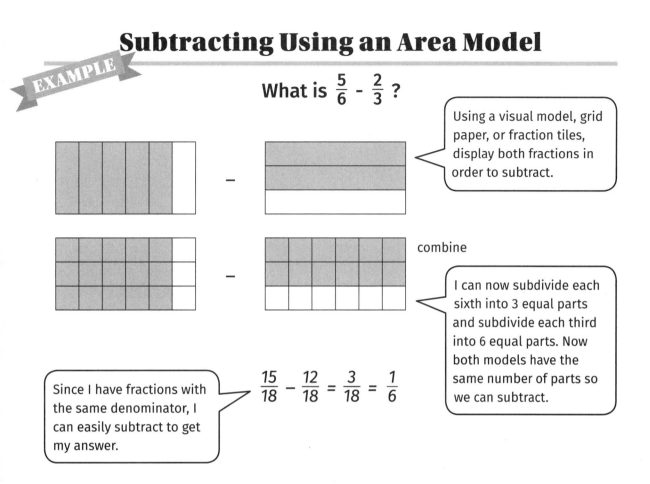

Using a visual model, grid paper, or fraction tiles, display both fractions in order to subtract.

combine

I can now subdivide each sixth into 3 equal parts and subdivide each third into 6 equal parts. Now both models have the same number of parts so we can subtract.

Since I have fractions with the same denominator, I can easily subtract to get my answer.

$$\frac{15}{18} - \frac{12}{18} = \frac{3}{18} = \frac{1}{6}$$

What is...?

$\frac{3}{4} - \frac{2}{6}$	$\frac{2}{4} - \frac{2}{6}$	$\frac{8}{12} - \frac{2}{4}$
$\frac{3}{4} - \frac{1}{5}$	$\frac{2}{5} - \frac{1}{4}$	$\frac{9}{12} - \frac{2}{3}$
$\frac{7}{9} - \frac{2}{3}$	$\frac{7}{12} - \frac{2}{4}$	$\frac{7}{8} - \frac{3}{4}$
$\frac{3}{5} - \frac{1}{3}$	$\frac{5}{6} - \frac{1}{3}$	$\frac{7}{12} - \frac{2}{4}$

Subtraction with Unit Fractions

What is $\frac{5}{6} - \frac{2}{3}$?

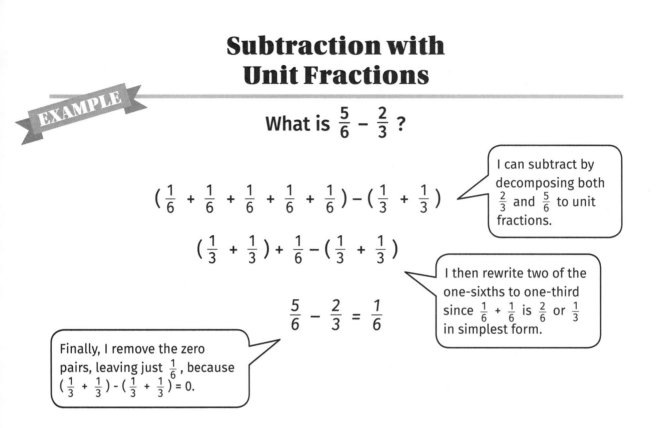

$(\frac{1}{6} + \frac{1}{6} + \frac{1}{6} + \frac{1}{6} + \frac{1}{6}) - (\frac{1}{3} + \frac{1}{3})$

I can subtract by decomposing both $\frac{2}{3}$ and $\frac{5}{6}$ to unit fractions.

$(\frac{1}{3} + \frac{1}{3}) + \frac{1}{6} - (\frac{1}{3} + \frac{1}{3})$

I then rewrite two of the one-sixths to one-third since $\frac{1}{6} + \frac{1}{6}$ is $\frac{2}{6}$ or $\frac{1}{3}$ in simplest form.

$\frac{5}{6} - \frac{2}{3} = \frac{1}{6}$

Finally, I remove the zero pairs, leaving just $\frac{1}{6}$, because $(\frac{1}{3} + \frac{1}{3}) - (\frac{1}{3} + \frac{1}{3}) = 0$.

What is...?

$\frac{3}{4} - \frac{1}{8}$	$\frac{2}{4} - \frac{3}{8}$	$\frac{2}{5} - \frac{1}{10}$
$\frac{6}{7} - \frac{3}{14}$	$\frac{2}{5} - \frac{3}{15}$	$\frac{3}{7} - \frac{1}{14}$
$\frac{8}{9} - \frac{2}{3}$	$\frac{7}{12} - \frac{2}{6}$	$\frac{7}{9} - \frac{2}{3}$
$\frac{3}{5} - \frac{3}{10}$	$\frac{5}{6} - \frac{1}{2}$	$\frac{1}{4} - \frac{1}{8}$

Subtracting Friendly Fractions

EXAMPLE

What is $\frac{17}{6} - \frac{5}{6}$?

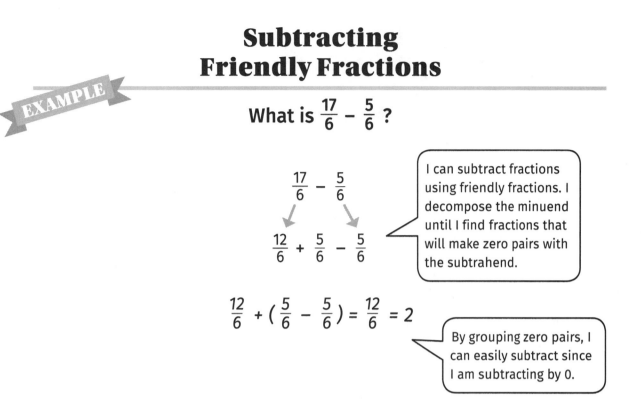

$$\frac{17}{6} - \frac{5}{6}$$

$$\frac{12}{6} + \frac{5}{6} - \frac{5}{6}$$

I can subtract fractions using friendly fractions. I decompose the minuend until I find fractions that will make zero pairs with the subtrahend.

$$\frac{12}{6} + \left(\frac{5}{6} - \frac{5}{6} \right) = \frac{12}{6} = 2$$

By grouping zero pairs, I can easily subtract since I am subtracting by 0.

What is…?

$\frac{9}{4} - \frac{5}{4}$	$\frac{2}{4} - \frac{3}{8}$	$\frac{2}{5} - \frac{1}{10}$
$\frac{3}{5} - \frac{1}{5}$	$\frac{2}{5} - \frac{3}{15}$	$\frac{3}{7} - \frac{1}{14}$
$\frac{8}{9} - \frac{3}{9}$	$\frac{7}{12} - \frac{2}{6}$	$\frac{7}{9} - \frac{2}{3}$
$\frac{3}{5} - \frac{3}{10}$	$\frac{5}{6} - \frac{1}{2}$	$\frac{1}{4} - \frac{1}{8}$

Subtracting Using Equivalent Fractions

What is $\frac{2}{3} - \frac{1}{8}$?

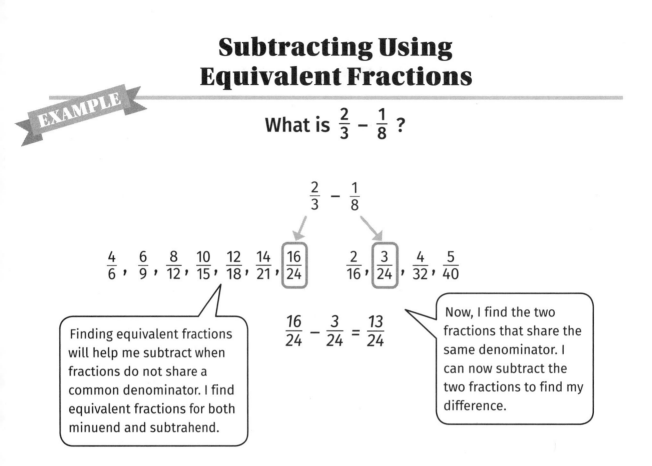

$$\frac{2}{3} - \frac{1}{8}$$

$$\frac{4}{6}, \frac{6}{9}, \frac{8}{12}, \frac{10}{15}, \frac{12}{18}, \frac{14}{21}, \boxed{\frac{16}{24}} \qquad \frac{2}{16}, \boxed{\frac{3}{24}}, \frac{4}{32}, \frac{5}{40}$$

$$\frac{16}{24} - \frac{3}{24} = \frac{13}{24}$$

Finding equivalent fractions will help me subtract when fractions do not share a common denominator. I find equivalent fractions for both minuend and subtrahend.

Now, I find the two fractions that share the same denominator. I can now subtract the two fractions to find my difference.

What is...?

$\frac{3}{4} - \frac{1}{5}$	$\frac{2}{4} - \frac{1}{5}$	$\frac{2}{5} - \frac{1}{4}$
$\frac{2}{7} - \frac{3}{4}$	$\frac{2}{5} - \frac{2}{7}$	$\frac{3}{7} - \frac{1}{5}$
$\frac{2}{9} - \frac{1}{3}$	$\frac{1}{12} - \frac{4}{6}$	$\frac{2}{9} - \frac{5}{6}$
$\frac{2}{5} - \frac{3}{6}$	$\frac{1}{6} - \frac{3}{8}$	$\frac{1}{5} - \frac{3}{8}$

Multiplying Using a Number Line

What is $4 \times \frac{1}{3}$?

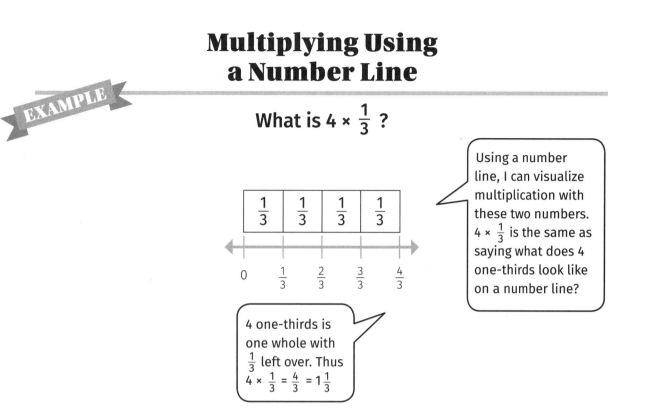

Using a number line, I can visualize multiplication with these two numbers. $4 \times \frac{1}{3}$ is the same as saying what does 4 one-thirds look like on a number line?

4 one-thirds is one whole with $\frac{1}{3}$ left over. Thus $4 \times \frac{1}{3} = \frac{4}{3} = 1\frac{1}{3}$

What is...?

$5 \times \frac{1}{5}$	$3 \times \frac{2}{8}$	$\frac{3}{4} \times 2$
$4 \times \frac{2}{3}$	$3 \times \frac{1}{7}$	$\frac{3}{10} \times 4$
$2 \times \frac{5}{8}$	$4 \times \frac{2}{3}$	$\frac{4}{7} \times 3$
$3 \times \frac{5}{6}$	$2 \times \frac{5}{9}$	$\frac{5}{8} \times 3$

Part-Whole

What is $\frac{3}{4}$ × 12 ?

Natalie has 12 books. She wants to return $\frac{3}{4}$ of the books to the library. How many will she return?

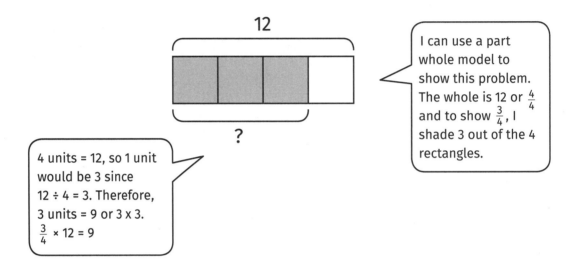

12

?

I can use a part whole model to show this problem. The whole is 12 or $\frac{4}{4}$ and to show $\frac{3}{4}$, I shade 3 out of the 4 rectangles.

4 units = 12, so 1 unit would be 3 since 12 ÷ 4 = 3. Therefore, 3 units = 9 or 3 x 3. $\frac{3}{4}$ × 12 = 9

What is...?

$\frac{2}{5}$ × 10	$\frac{2}{9}$ × 9	$\frac{3}{4}$ × 12
$\frac{2}{8}$ × 24	$\frac{2}{3}$ × 12	$\frac{3}{10}$ × 20
$\frac{3}{4}$ × 8	$\frac{4}{7}$ × 21	$\frac{4}{7}$ × 7
$\frac{5}{6}$ × 12	$\frac{1}{4}$ × 16	$\frac{5}{8}$ × 16

Using a Tape Diagram

What is $\frac{1}{3} \times \frac{1}{5}$?

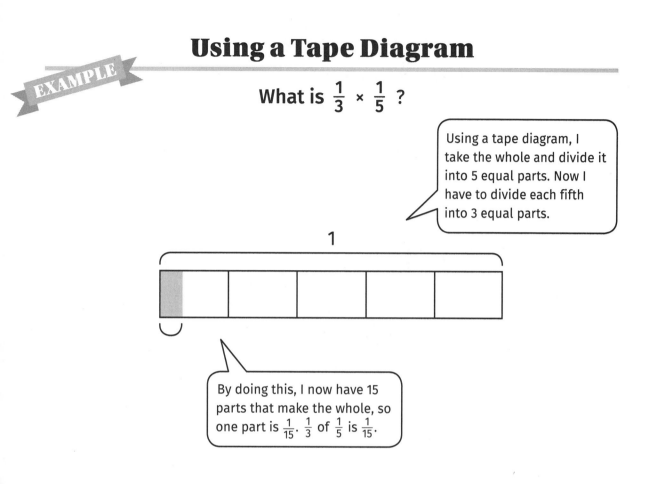

Using a tape diagram, I take the whole and divide it into 5 equal parts. Now I have to divide each fifth into 3 equal parts.

1

By doing this, I now have 15 parts that make the whole, so one part is $\frac{1}{15}$. $\frac{1}{3}$ of $\frac{1}{5}$ is $\frac{1}{15}$.

What is...?

$\frac{1}{5} \times \frac{1}{4}$	$\frac{1}{2} \times \frac{1}{6}$	$\frac{1}{4} \times \frac{1}{3}$
$\frac{1}{8} \times \frac{1}{2}$	$\frac{1}{3} \times \frac{1}{6}$	$\frac{1}{10} \times \frac{1}{2}$
$\frac{1}{4} \times \frac{1}{4}$	$\frac{1}{7} \times \frac{1}{2}$	$\frac{1}{7} \times \frac{1}{3}$
$\frac{1}{6} \times \frac{1}{4}$	$\frac{1}{4} \times \frac{1}{2}$	$\frac{1}{8} \times \frac{1}{2}$

Area Model
(Fraction × Fraction)

What is $\frac{3}{4} \times \frac{1}{2}$?

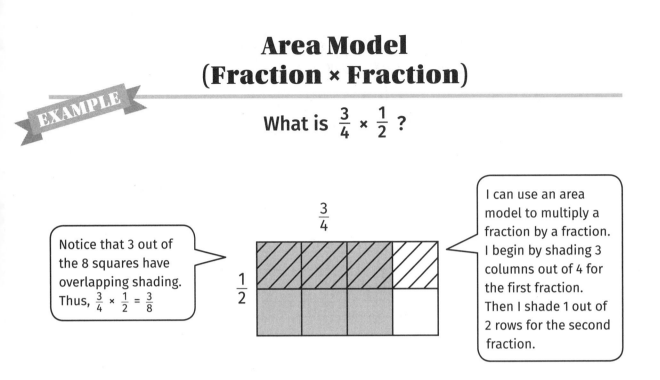

Notice that 3 out of the 8 squares have overlapping shading. Thus, $\frac{3}{4} \times \frac{1}{2} = \frac{3}{8}$

I can use an area model to multiply a fraction by a fraction. I begin by shading 3 columns out of 4 for the first fraction. Then I shade 1 out of 2 rows for the second fraction.

What is...?

$\frac{3}{4} \times \frac{1}{3}$	$\frac{3}{5} \times \frac{2}{3}$	$\frac{2}{6} \times \frac{3}{8}$
$\frac{1}{4} \times \frac{8}{9}$	$\frac{3}{8} \times \frac{2}{3}$	$\frac{1}{7} \times \frac{2}{5}$
$\frac{2}{3} \times \frac{1}{4}$	$\frac{3}{4} \times \frac{2}{3}$	$\frac{4}{6} \times \frac{1}{3}$
$\frac{1}{4} \times \frac{2}{5}$	$\frac{2}{5} \times \frac{3}{4}$	$\frac{2}{9} \times \frac{1}{2}$

Area Model
with Mixed Numbers

What is $2\frac{1}{2} \times 4\frac{3}{4}$?

	2	$\frac{1}{2}$
4	$4 \times 2 = 8$	$4 \times \frac{1}{2} = \frac{4}{2} = 2$
$\frac{3}{4}$	$\frac{3}{4} \times 2 = \frac{6}{4} = 1\frac{1}{2}$	$\frac{3}{4} \times \frac{1}{2} = \frac{3}{8}$

I can use an area model to multiply mixed numbers. I can find each partial product by first multiplying 4×2, then $4 \times \frac{1}{2}$.

Next I multiply $\frac{3}{4}$ by 2 and by $\frac{1}{2}$. Finally, to get my product, I add the partial products.

$$8 + 2 + 1\frac{1}{2} + \frac{3}{8} = 11\frac{7}{8}$$

What is...?

$1\frac{1}{2} \times 3\frac{1}{3}$	$7\frac{1}{2} \times 4\frac{1}{4}$	$4\frac{3}{5} \times 2\frac{2}{3}$
$6\frac{3}{4} \times 5\frac{2}{7}$	$4\frac{4}{6} \times 3\frac{1}{3}$	$2\frac{2}{5} \times 5\frac{3}{4}$
$3\frac{1}{3} \times 4\frac{3}{4}$	$2\frac{2}{5} \times 1\frac{3}{10}$	$3\frac{1}{8} \times 2\frac{1}{4}$
$6\frac{1}{2} \times 3\frac{2}{5}$	$8\frac{4}{5} \times \frac{3}{4}$	$5\frac{2}{6} \times 2\frac{2}{3}$

Rounding and Compensating

What is $5 \times 4\frac{3}{4}$?

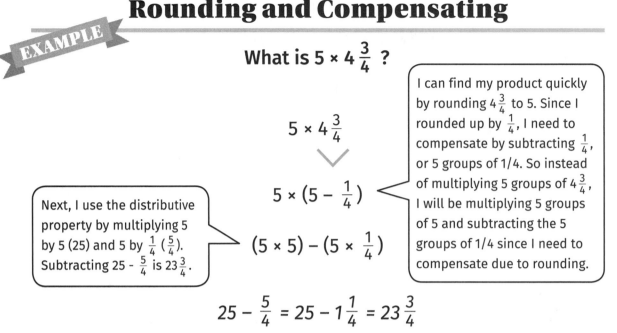

$5 \times 4\frac{3}{4}$

I can find my product quickly by rounding $4\frac{3}{4}$ to 5. Since I rounded up by $\frac{1}{4}$, I need to compensate by subtracting $\frac{1}{4}$, or 5 groups of 1/4. So instead of multiplying 5 groups of $4\frac{3}{4}$, I will be multiplying 5 groups of 5 and subtracting the 5 groups of 1/4 since I need to compensate due to rounding.

$5 \times (5 - \frac{1}{4})$

Next, I use the distributive property by multiplying 5 by 5 (25) and 5 by $\frac{1}{4}$ ($\frac{5}{4}$). Subtracting $25 - \frac{5}{4}$ is $23\frac{3}{4}$.

$(5 \times 5) - (5 \times \frac{1}{4})$

$$25 - \frac{5}{4} = 25 - 1\frac{1}{4} = 23\frac{3}{4}$$

What is...?

$3 \times 3\frac{2}{3}$	$7 \times 4\frac{3}{4}$	$4 \times 2\frac{2}{3}$
$2 \times 3\frac{5}{6}$	$5 \times 3\frac{2}{3}$	$2 \times 5\frac{3}{4}$
$4 \times 4\frac{3}{4}$	$2 \times 1\frac{9}{10}$	$3 \times 2\frac{4}{5}$
$6 \times 3\frac{4}{5}$	$8 \times 2\frac{3}{4}$	$5 \times 2\frac{4}{5}$

Division with Fraction Tiles

What is $\frac{5}{8} \div \frac{1}{4}$?

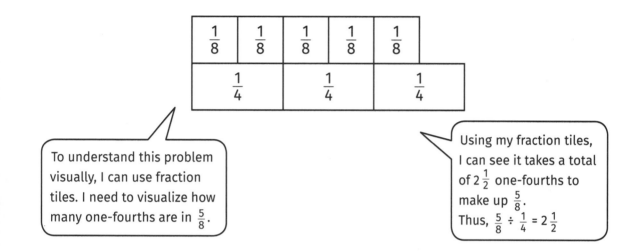

To understand this problem visually, I can use fraction tiles. I need to visualize how many one-fourths are in $\frac{5}{8}$.

Using my fraction tiles, I can see it takes a total of $2\frac{1}{2}$ one-fourths to make up $\frac{5}{8}$.
Thus, $\frac{5}{8} \div \frac{1}{4} = 2\frac{1}{2}$

What is...?

$\frac{2}{3} \div \frac{2}{12}$	$\frac{3}{5} \div \frac{1}{7}$	$\frac{3}{4} \div \frac{1}{4}$
$\frac{3}{4} \div \frac{2}{12}$	$\frac{1}{2} \div \frac{1}{10}$	$\frac{1}{4} \div \frac{2}{8}$
$\frac{9}{12} \div \frac{1}{4}$	$\frac{6}{12} \div \frac{1}{4}$	$\frac{4}{6} \div \frac{2}{9}$
$\frac{4}{6} \div \frac{2}{3}$	$\frac{4}{6} \div \frac{2}{12}$	$\frac{1}{2} \div \frac{2}{12}$

Fractions and Whole Numbers

EXAMPLE

What is $\frac{1}{3} \div 4$?

I can solve this division problem by partitioning a rectangle into 3 parts, shading $\frac{1}{3}$ of the whole.

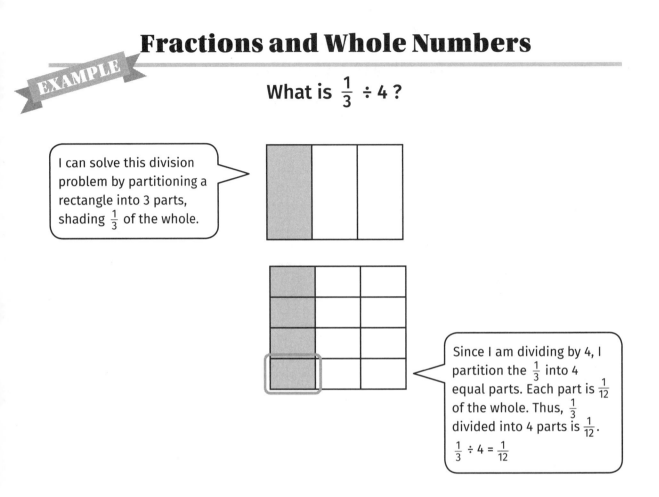

Since I am dividing by 4, I partition the $\frac{1}{3}$ into 4 equal parts. Each part is $\frac{1}{12}$ of the whole. Thus, $\frac{1}{3}$ divided into 4 parts is $\frac{1}{12}$.

$\frac{1}{3} \div 4 = \frac{1}{12}$

What is...?

$\frac{2}{3} \div 4$	$\frac{3}{5} \div 2$	$\frac{3}{4} \div 5$
$\frac{5}{12} \div 2$	$\frac{2}{9} \div 2$	$\frac{1}{4} \div 5$
$\frac{2}{4} \div 6$	$\frac{3}{5} \div 3$	$\frac{4}{6} \div 3$
$\frac{7}{8} \div 2$	$\frac{5}{8} \div 3$	$\frac{1}{2} \div 8$

Partitioning Whole Numbers by Unit Fractions

What is $5 \div \frac{1}{4}$?

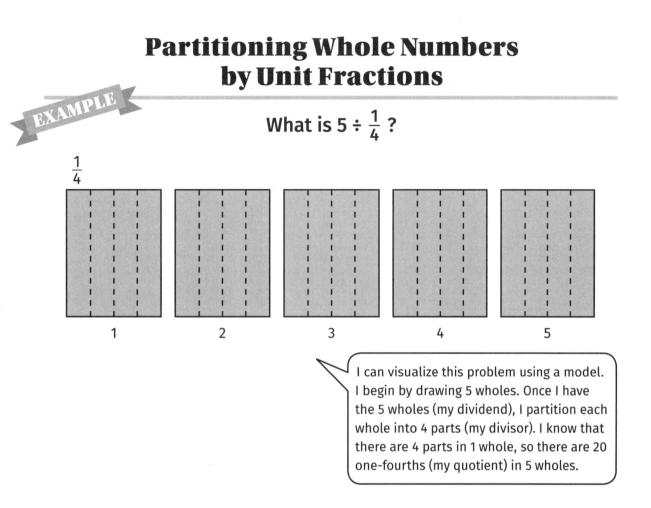

$\frac{1}{4}$

1   2   3   4   5

> I can visualize this problem using a model. I begin by drawing 5 wholes. Once I have the 5 wholes (my dividend), I partition each whole into 4 parts (my divisor). I know that there are 4 parts in 1 whole, so there are 20 one-fourths (my quotient) in 5 wholes.

What is...?

$6 \div \frac{1}{12}$	$2 \div \frac{1}{7}$	$3 \div \frac{1}{3}$
$5 \div \frac{1}{3}$	$4 \div \frac{1}{10}$	$7 \div \frac{1}{2}$
$5 \div \frac{1}{7}$	$7 \div 3$	$6 \div \frac{1}{9}$
$2 \div \frac{1}{5}$	$8 \div \frac{1}{2}$	$2 \div \frac{1}{9}$

Partitioning Unit Fractions by a Whole Number

What is $\frac{1}{5} \div 3$?

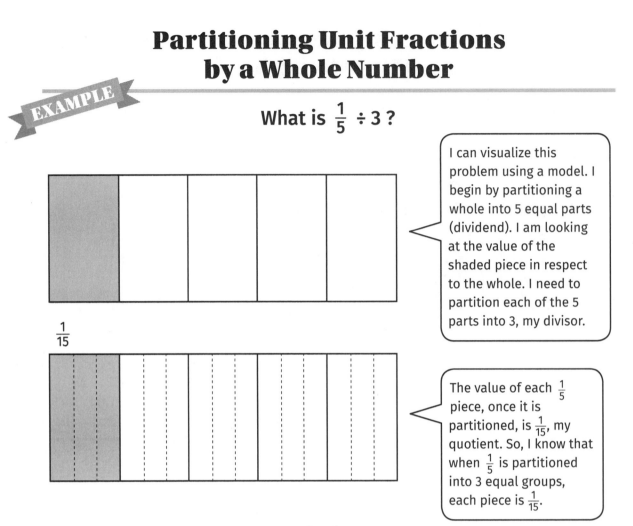

I can visualize this problem using a model. I begin by partitioning a whole into 5 equal parts (dividend). I am looking at the value of the shaded piece in respect to the whole. I need to partition each of the 5 parts into 3, my divisor.

$\frac{1}{15}$

The value of each $\frac{1}{5}$ piece, once it is partitioned, is $\frac{1}{15}$, my quotient. So, I know that when $\frac{1}{5}$ is partitioned into 3 equal groups, each piece is $\frac{1}{15}$.

What is...?

$\frac{1}{10} \div 2$	$\frac{1}{4} \div 4$	$\frac{1}{2} \div 4$
$\frac{1}{5} \div 6$	$\frac{1}{5} \div 2$	$\frac{1}{4} \div 3$
$\frac{1}{6} \div 3$	$\frac{1}{6} \div 4$	$\frac{1}{9} \div 2$
$\frac{1}{4} \div 2$	$\frac{1}{4} \div 6$	$\frac{1}{7} \div 4$

Number Lines (Unit Fraction and Whole Number)

What is $\frac{1}{5} \div 3$?

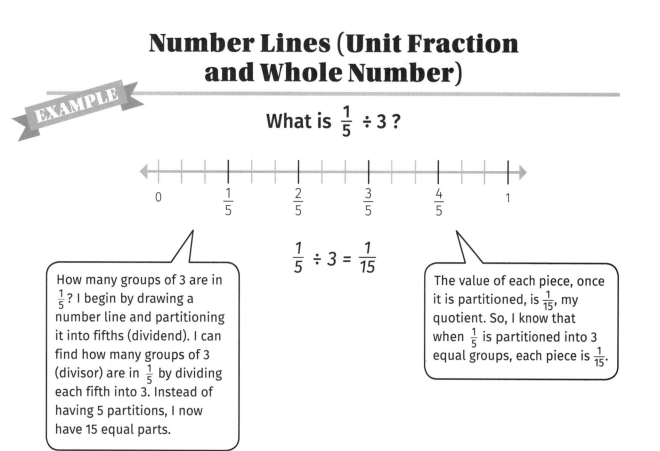

$$\frac{1}{5} \div 3 = \frac{1}{15}$$

How many groups of 3 are in $\frac{1}{5}$? I begin by drawing a number line and partitioning it into fifths (dividend). I can find how many groups of 3 (divisor) are in $\frac{1}{5}$ by dividing each fifth into 3. Instead of having 5 partitions, I now have 15 equal parts.

The value of each piece, once it is partitioned, is $\frac{1}{15}$, my quotient. So, I know that when $\frac{1}{5}$ is partitioned into 3 equal groups, each piece is $\frac{1}{15}$.

What is...?

$\frac{1}{8} \div 4$	$\frac{1}{4} \div 4$	$\frac{1}{2} \div 4$
$\frac{1}{5} \div 6$	$\frac{1}{5} \div 2$	$\frac{1}{4} \div 3$
$\frac{1}{6} \div 3$	$\frac{1}{6} \div 4$	$\frac{1}{9} \div 2$
$\frac{1}{4} \div 2$	$\frac{1}{4} \div 6$	$\frac{1}{7} \div 4$

Number Lines (Whole Number and Unit Fraction)

What is $3 \div \frac{1}{4}$?

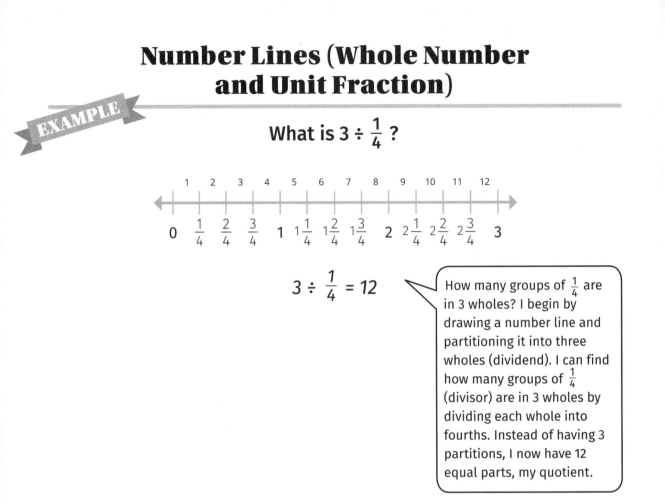

$$3 \div \frac{1}{4} = 12$$

> How many groups of $\frac{1}{4}$ are in 3 wholes? I begin by drawing a number line and partitioning it into three wholes (dividend). I can find how many groups of $\frac{1}{4}$ (divisor) are in 3 wholes by dividing each whole into fourths. Instead of having 3 partitions, I now have 12 equal parts, my quotient.

What is...?

$6 \div \frac{1}{12}$	$2 \div \frac{1}{7}$	$3 \div \frac{1}{3}$
$5 \div \frac{1}{3}$	$4 \div \frac{1}{10}$	$7 \div \frac{1}{2}$
$5 \div \frac{1}{7}$	$7 \div \frac{1}{3}$	$6 \div \frac{1}{9}$
$2 \div \frac{1}{5}$	$8 \div \frac{1}{2}$	$2 \div \frac{1}{9}$

Number Lines (Fraction Divided by a Fraction)

What is $\frac{7}{8} \div \frac{1}{4}$?

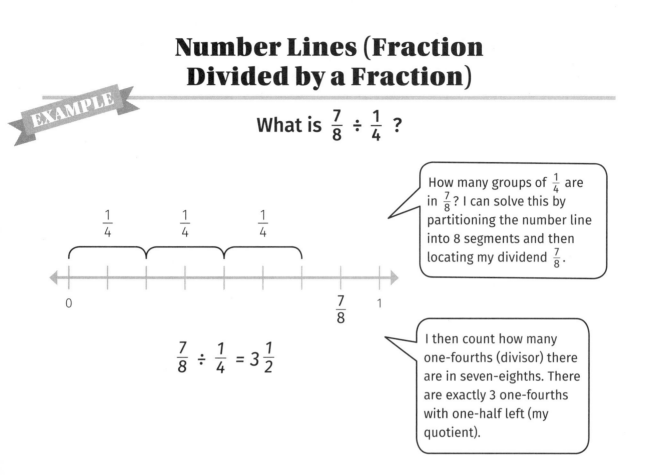

How many groups of $\frac{1}{4}$ are in $\frac{7}{8}$? I can solve this by partitioning the number line into 8 segments and then locating my dividend $\frac{7}{8}$.

$$\frac{7}{8} \div \frac{1}{4} = 3\frac{1}{2}$$

I then count how many one-fourths (divisor) there are in seven-eighths. There are exactly 3 one-fourths with one-half left (my quotient).

What is...?

$\frac{5}{6} \div \frac{1}{3}$	$\frac{3}{5} \div \frac{1}{10}$	$\frac{3}{6} \div \frac{1}{4}$
$\frac{8}{12} \div \frac{2}{3}$	$\frac{6}{9} \div \frac{2}{6}$	$\frac{9}{12} \div \frac{1}{2}$
$\frac{2}{4} \div \frac{1}{8}$	$\frac{3}{4} \div \frac{1}{2}$	$\frac{4}{6} \div \frac{1}{3}$
$\frac{7}{10} \div \frac{2}{5}$	$\frac{5}{8} \div \frac{1}{4}$	$\frac{5}{10} \div \frac{1}{2}$

Using a Tape Diagram

What is $\frac{7}{8} \div \frac{1}{4}$?

> How many groups of $\frac{1}{4}$ are in $\frac{7}{8}$? I can solve this problem by partitioning the shape into 8 segments and then shading 7 out of the 8 (dividend).

1	1	1	$\frac{1}{2}$

> Counting how many one-fourths there are in $\frac{7}{8}$ will give me my quotient. There are exactly 3 one-fourths with $\frac{1}{2}$ left in $\frac{7}{8}$. Thus, $\frac{7}{8} \div \frac{1}{4} = 3\frac{1}{2}$.

What is...?

$\frac{5}{8} \div \frac{1}{4}$	$\frac{2}{5} \div \frac{1}{10}$	$\frac{1}{2} \div \frac{4}{16}$
$\frac{7}{10} \div \frac{1}{5}$	$\frac{6}{9} \div \frac{2}{3}$	$\frac{8}{12} \div \frac{2}{3}$
$\frac{3}{4} \div \frac{1}{8}$	$\frac{2}{4} \div \frac{1}{8}$	$\frac{4}{8} \div \frac{1}{2}$
$\frac{3}{8} \div \frac{1}{16}$	$\frac{6}{8} \div \frac{2}{16}$	$\frac{6}{10} \div \frac{1}{5}$

Dividing with Fraction Tiles

What is $\frac{5}{8} \div \frac{1}{4}$?

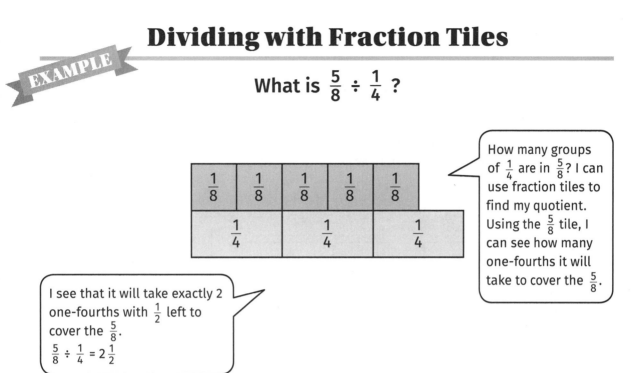

How many groups of $\frac{1}{4}$ are in $\frac{5}{8}$? I can use fraction tiles to find my quotient. Using the $\frac{5}{8}$ tile, I can see how many one-fourths it will take to cover the $\frac{5}{8}$.

I see that it will take exactly 2 one-fourths with $\frac{1}{2}$ left to cover the $\frac{5}{8}$.

$\frac{5}{8} \div \frac{1}{4} = 2\frac{1}{2}$

What is...?

$\frac{2}{3} \div \frac{1}{9}$	$\frac{1}{2} \div \frac{1}{4}$	$\frac{6}{12} \div \frac{1}{4}$
$\frac{5}{6} \div \frac{1}{3}$	$\frac{6}{9} \div \frac{1}{3}$	$\frac{9}{12} \div \frac{1}{4}$
$\frac{1}{4} \div \frac{1}{8}$	$\frac{3}{4} \div \frac{1}{4}$	$\frac{2}{6} \div \frac{1}{9}$
$\frac{8}{10} \div \frac{2}{5}$	$\frac{3}{4} \div \frac{1}{12}$	$\frac{8}{10} \div \frac{1}{5}$

Double Bar Model

What is $\frac{2}{3} \div \frac{1}{6}$?

Mike solved math problems for $\frac{2}{3}$ of an hour. It takes him $\frac{1}{6}$ hour to solve one problem. How many problems has Mike solved?

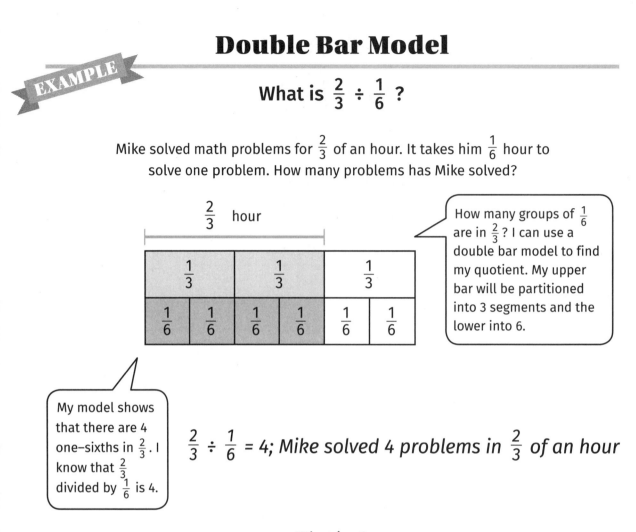

$\frac{2}{3}$ hour

| $\frac{1}{3}$ | $\frac{1}{3}$ | $\frac{1}{3}$ |

| $\frac{1}{6}$ | $\frac{1}{6}$ | $\frac{1}{6}$ | $\frac{1}{6}$ | $\frac{1}{6}$ | $\frac{1}{6}$ |

How many groups of $\frac{1}{6}$ are in $\frac{2}{3}$? I can use a double bar model to find my quotient. My upper bar will be partitioned into 3 segments and the lower into 6.

My model shows that there are 4 one–sixths in $\frac{2}{3}$. I know that $\frac{2}{3}$ divided by $\frac{1}{6}$ is 4.

$\frac{2}{3} \div \frac{1}{6} = 4$; *Mike solved 4 problems in $\frac{2}{3}$ of an hour*

What is...?

$\frac{1}{3} \div \frac{1}{15}$	$\frac{1}{2} \div \frac{2}{8}$	$\frac{8}{12} \div \frac{1}{6}$
$\frac{4}{6} \div \frac{1}{3}$	$\frac{3}{9} \div \frac{1}{3}$	$\frac{4}{12} \div \frac{1}{9}$
$\frac{3}{4} \div \frac{3}{8}$	$\frac{5}{4} \div \frac{1}{2}$	$\frac{4}{6} \div \frac{2}{18}$
$\frac{8}{10} \div \frac{1}{5}$	$\frac{1}{4} \div \frac{1}{8}$	$\frac{12}{10} \div \frac{1}{5}$

Area Model

What is $\frac{2}{3} \div \frac{3}{4}$?

How many $\frac{3}{4}$ cup servings are in $\frac{2}{3}$ cup of yogurt?

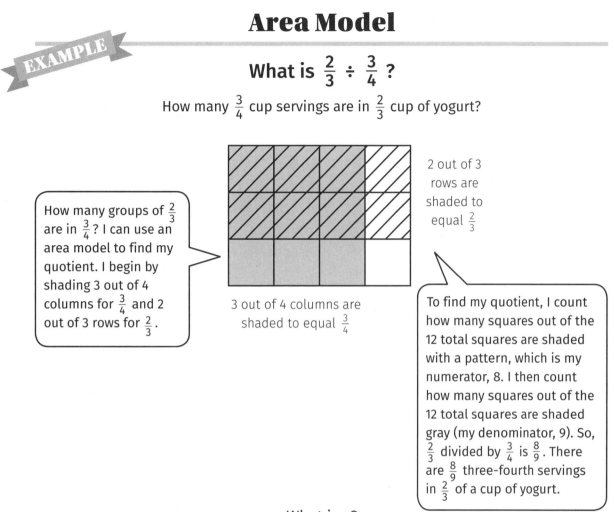

How many groups of $\frac{2}{3}$ are in $\frac{3}{4}$? I can use an area model to find my quotient. I begin by shading 3 out of 4 columns for $\frac{3}{4}$ and 2 out of 3 rows for $\frac{2}{3}$.

2 out of 3 rows are shaded to equal $\frac{2}{3}$

3 out of 4 columns are shaded to equal $\frac{3}{4}$

To find my quotient, I count how many squares out of the 12 total squares are shaded with a pattern, which is my numerator, 8. I then count how many squares out of the 12 total squares are shaded gray (my denominator, 9). So, $\frac{2}{3}$ divided by $\frac{3}{4}$ is $\frac{8}{9}$. There are $\frac{8}{9}$ three-fourth servings in $\frac{2}{3}$ of a cup of yogurt.

What is...?

$\frac{1}{3} \div \frac{1}{15}$	$\frac{1}{2} \div \frac{2}{8}$	$\frac{8}{12} \div \frac{1}{6}$
$\frac{4}{6} \div \frac{1}{3}$	$\frac{3}{9} \div \frac{1}{3}$	$\frac{4}{12} \div \frac{1}{9}$
$\frac{3}{4} \div \frac{3}{8}$	$\frac{5}{4} \div \frac{1}{2}$	$\frac{4}{6} \div \frac{2}{18}$
$\frac{8}{10} \div \frac{1}{5}$	$\frac{1}{4} \div \frac{1}{8}$	$\frac{12}{10} \div \frac{1}{5}$

Dividing Across Numerator/ Denominator

What is $\frac{6}{8} \div \frac{1}{4}$?

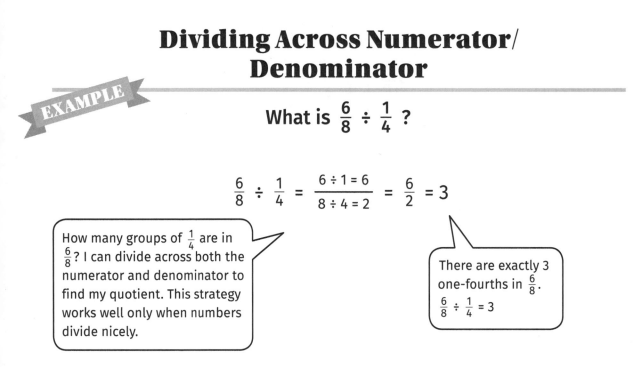

$$\frac{6}{8} \div \frac{1}{4} = \frac{6 \div 1 = 6}{8 \div 4 = 2} = \frac{6}{2} = 3$$

How many groups of $\frac{1}{4}$ are in $\frac{6}{8}$? I can divide across both the numerator and denominator to find my quotient. This strategy works well only when numbers divide nicely.

There are exactly 3 one-fourths in $\frac{6}{8}$.
$\frac{6}{8} \div \frac{1}{4} = 3$

What is...?

$\frac{12}{28} \div \frac{6}{7}$	$\frac{8}{12} \div \frac{4}{24}$	$\frac{6}{12} \div \frac{2}{6}$
$\frac{4}{8} \div \frac{2}{16}$	$\frac{6}{9} \div \frac{2}{3}$	$\frac{9}{12} \div \frac{3}{4}$
$\frac{12}{4} \div \frac{3}{4}$	$\frac{3}{16} \div \frac{1}{4}$	$\frac{12}{6} \div \frac{6}{3}$
$\frac{7}{10} \div \frac{7}{2}$	$\frac{6}{8} \div \frac{3}{4}$	$\frac{8}{10} \div \frac{4}{2}$

Decimal Strategies

Adding Decimals on an Open Number Line

What is 3.25 + 4.37?

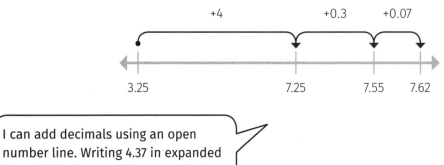

I can add decimals using an open number line. Writing 4.37 in expanded form will help me add on a number line. 4.37 in expanded form is 4 + 0.3 + 0.07. I begin at 3.25, I then jump 4 whole numbers to 7.25, I then jump 3 tenths more to 7.55, and finally I jump 7 hundredths to 7.62, my answer.

What is...?

0.99 + 0.24	1.89 + 1.62	5.82 + 2.64
4.46 + 2.85	6.37 + 4.21	8.54 + 7.65
1.11 + 5.39	3.71 + 3.58	1.16 + 0.45
8.89 + 3.42	5.25 + 7.12	3.82 + 3.71

Adding on Tenths and Hundredths

What is 4.34 + 2.32?

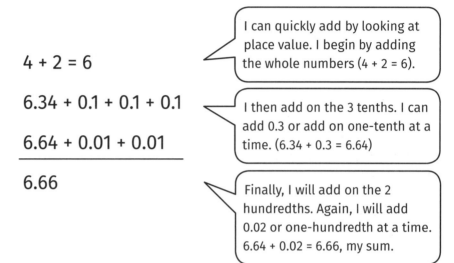

4 + 2 = 6

I can quickly add by looking at place value. I begin by adding the whole numbers (4 + 2 = 6).

6.34 + 0.1 + 0.1 + 0.1

I then add on the 3 tenths. I can add 0.3 or add on one-tenth at a time. (6.34 + 0.3 = 6.64)

6.64 + 0.01 + 0.01
─────────────────
6.66

Finally, I will add on the 2 hundredths. Again, I will add 0.02 or one-hundredth at a time. 6.64 + 0.02 = 6.66, my sum.

What is...?

3.09 + 1.32	6.83 + 2.22	4.48 + 3.26
5.67 + 4.04	9.56 + 1.34	7.42 + 2.31
72.45 + 21.41	32.63 + 21.14	62.43 + 20.42
25.62 + 30.25	28.65 + 13.34	56.53 + 31.44

Decomposing

What is 7.42 + 8.75?

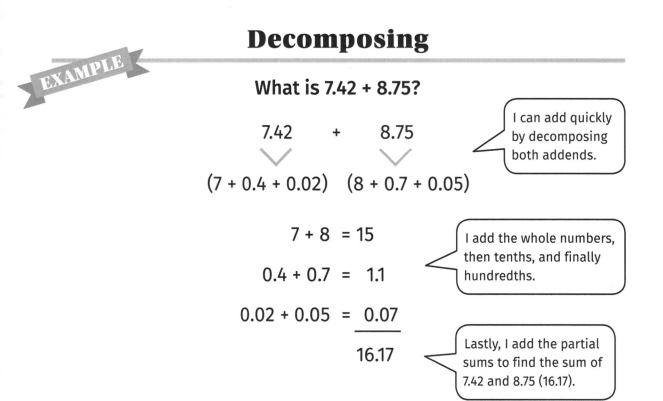

$$7.42 \quad + \quad 8.75$$

$$(7 + 0.4 + 0.02) \quad (8 + 0.7 + 0.05)$$

I can add quickly by decomposing both addends.

$$7 + 8 = 15$$

$$0.4 + 0.7 = 1.1$$

$$0.02 + 0.05 = \underline{0.07}$$

$$16.17$$

I add the whole numbers, then tenths, and finally hundredths.

Lastly, I add the partial sums to find the sum of 7.42 and 8.75 (16.17).

What is...?

8.53 + 3.45	3.21 + 4.05	1.17 + 3.41
1.45 + 1.32	45.6 + 32.47	30.21 + 4.19
6.72 + 5.45	32.46 + 1.23	22.32 + 4.56
9.52 + 7.32	10.63 + 4.24	12.34 + 8.53

Using Place Value

What is 10.48 + 5.32?

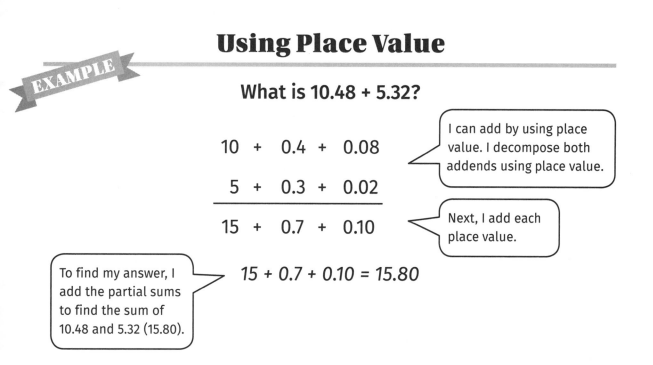

10 + 0.4 + 0.08

5 + 0.3 + 0.02

_____

15 + 0.7 + 0.10

I can add by using place value. I decompose both addends using place value.

Next, I add each place value.

To find my answer, I add the partial sums to find the sum of 10.48 and 5.32 (15.80).

$15 + 0.7 + 0.10 = 15.80$

What is...?

12.34 + 6.45	15.42 + 9.37	14.34 + 8.62
42.5 + 31.28	1.08 + 0.42	12.1 + 10.91
0.38 + 11.3	1.46 + 0.33	1.86 + 0.32
123.45 + 34.24	325.31 + 124.46	457.42 + 32.36

Adding Left to Right

What is 13.45 + 6.28?

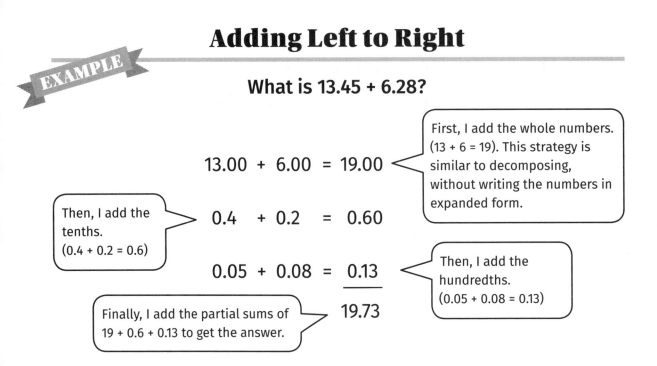

13.00 + 6.00 = 19.00

First, I add the whole numbers. (13 + 6 = 19). This strategy is similar to decomposing, without writing the numbers in expanded form.

Then, I add the tenths. (0.4 + 0.2 = 0.6)

0.4 + 0.2 = 0.60

0.05 + 0.08 = 0.13

Then, I add the hundredths. (0.05 + 0.08 = 0.13)

Finally, I add the partial sums of 19 + 0.6 + 0.13 to get the answer.

19.73

What is...?

15.63 + 12.34	3.21 + 4.05	1.17 + 3.41
25.63 + 9.48	45.6 + 32.47	30.21 + 4.19
28.39 + 11.52	32.46 + 1.23	22.32 + 4.56
11.48 + 14.38	10.63 + 4.24	12.34 + 8.53

Rounding the Subtrahend/ Compensating

What is 5.87 – 2.98?

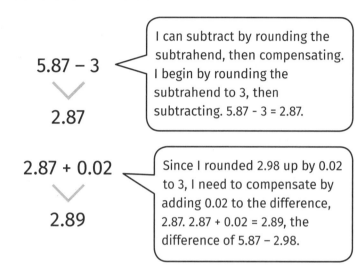

5.87 – 3

2.87

> I can subtract by rounding the subtrahend, then compensating. I begin by rounding the subtrahend to 3, then subtracting. 5.87 - 3 = 2.87.

2.87 + 0.02

2.89

> Since I rounded 2.98 up by 0.02 to 3, I need to compensate by adding 0.02 to the difference, 2.87. 2.87 + 0.02 = 2.89, the difference of 5.87 – 2.98.

What is...?

1.76 – 0.87	7.72 – 3.97	6.56 – 3.96
5.87 – 3.94	5.87 – 2.92	7.48 – 4.99
6.78 – 4.88	6.96 – 4.91	8.58 – 6.94
3.5 – 1.96	8.59 – 5.89	4.48 – 2.88

Adding Up to Subtract on an Open Number Line

What is 5.67 – 3.39?

I can subtract these two numbers by adding up to friendly numbers on a number line. I begin on an open number line at the subtrahend, 3.39. I add 0.01 to jump to 3.40. Then, I can add 0.60 to jump to 4.00, then 1.00 for a jump to 5.00, and then another 0.67 to get to the minuend, 5.67. So, I know the distance or difference between the two numbers is 0.01 + 0.60 + 1.00 + 0.67, or 2.28.

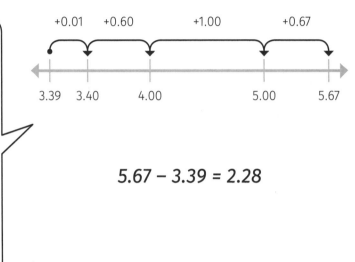

$$5.67 - 3.39 = 2.28$$

What is...?

7.67 – 4.69	7.45 – 5.25	8.81 – 6.74
8.39 – 2.89	8.85 – 6.98	9.38 – 7.42
1.76 – 0.58	4.49 – 2.65	5.53 – 3.88
6.14 – 3.67	3.59 – 1.75	7.12 – 6.98

Subtracting Down on an Open Number Line

What is 8.98 − 6.23?

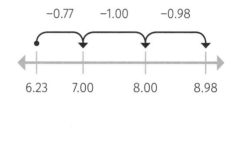

I can subtract down on an open number line using friendly numbers to find my difference. I begin on an open number line at the minuend 8.98. I jump back 0.98 to 8.00, then another 1.00 to get to 7.00. I know that 23 and 77 is 100, so I can jump back 0.77 to get to 6.23, the subtrahend. To find the difference or distance between the two numbers, I add 0.77 + 1.00 + 0.98 to get 2.75

8.98 − 6.23 = 2.75

What is...?

8.85 − 3.78	9.21 − 5.89	6.63 − 4.59
4.25 − 3.12	7.36 − 3.65	8.25 − 5.75
7.49 − 4.38	4.44 − 2.78	3.36 − 1.70
6.25 − 2.75	8.35 − 2.79	5.12 − 2.25

Place Value on an Open Number Line

What is 7.46 − 4.21 ?

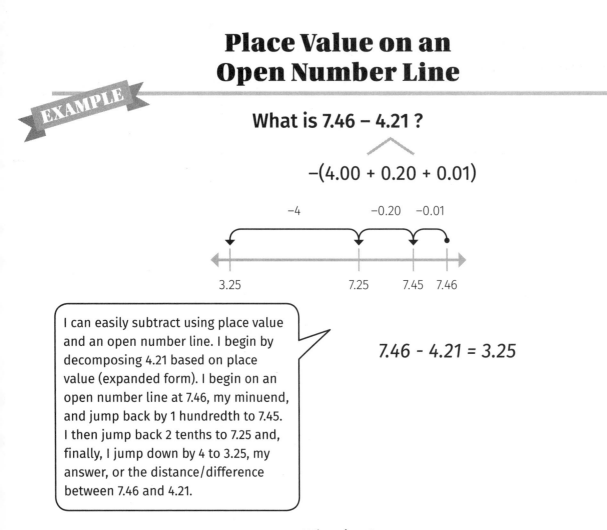

−(4.00 + 0.20 + 0.01)

I can easily subtract using place value and an open number line. I begin by decomposing 4.21 based on place value (expanded form). I begin on an open number line at 7.46, my minuend, and jump back by 1 hundredth to 7.45. I then jump back 2 tenths to 7.25 and, finally, I jump down by 4 to 3.25, my answer, or the distance/difference between 7.46 and 4.21.

7.46 − 4.21 = 3.25

What is...?

1.45 − 0.23	10.05 − 2.03	2.64 − 1.23
8.93 − 6.42	8.42 − 7.31	15.49 − 12.26
9.47 − 6.25	16.26 − 13.03	2.86 − 1.24
15.36 − 13.32	15.58 − 10.36	2.25 − 1.13

Adding for Same Difference on an Open Number Line

What is 5.67 – 2.99?

I can make subtraction easy by finding easy numbers to subtract. In this case, I can add 0.01 to both the subtrahend and minuend, giving me those easy numbers to subtract.

$(5.67 + 0.01) – (2.99 + 0.01)$

5.68   –   3.00

2.68

Now we have something easier to subtract, 5.68 and 3.00.

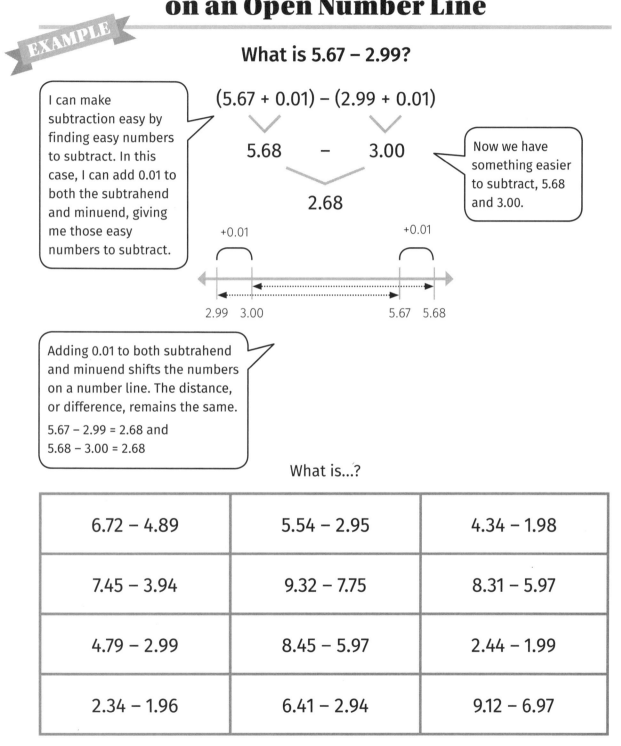

+0.01   +0.01

2.99 3.00   5.67 5.68

Adding 0.01 to both subtrahend and minuend shifts the numbers on a number line. The distance, or difference, remains the same.
5.67 – 2.99 = 2.68 and
5.68 – 3.00 = 2.68

What is...?

6.72 – 4.89	5.54 – 2.95	4.34 – 1.98
7.45 – 3.94	9.32 – 7.75	8.31 – 5.97
4.79 – 2.99	8.45 – 5.97	2.44 – 1.99
2.34 – 1.96	6.41 – 2.94	9.12 – 6.97

Subtracting for Same Distance
on an Open Number Line

What is 9.00 – 6.24?

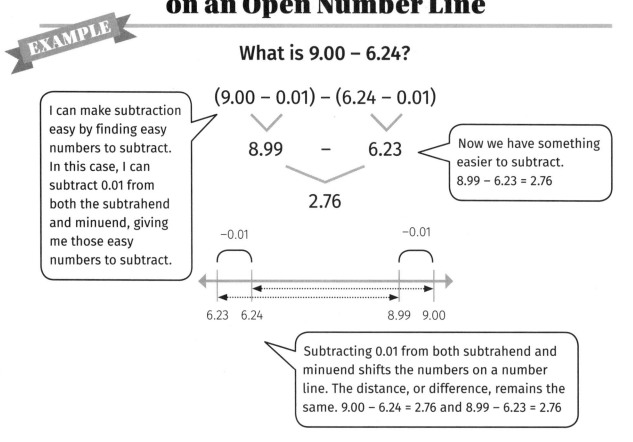

$(9.00 - 0.01) - (6.24 - 0.01)$

8.99   –   6.23

2.76

I can make subtraction easy by finding easy numbers to subtract. In this case, I can subtract 0.01 from both the subtrahend and minuend, giving me those easy numbers to subtract.

Now we have something easier to subtract.
8.99 – 6.23 = 2.76

−0.01   −0.01

6.23   6.24   8.99   9.00

Subtracting 0.01 from both subtrahend and minuend shifts the numbers on a number line. The distance, or difference, remains the same. 9.00 – 6.24 = 2.76 and 8.99 – 6.23 = 2.76

What is…?

10.00 − 5.67	3.00 − 2.13	8.00 − 5.87
5.00 − 2.53	4.00 − 1.76	6.00 − 3.97
7.00 − 5.34	9.00 − 7.23	2.00 − 0.82
3.00 − 1.56	8.00 − 3.87	7.00 − 2.95

Counting Back by Tenths and Hundredths

What is 10.58 − 5.32?

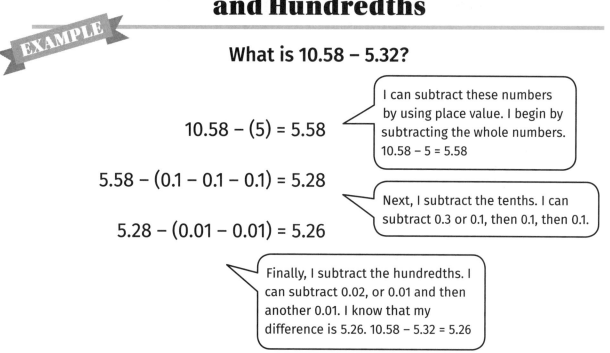

$$10.58 - (5) = 5.58$$

I can subtract these numbers by using place value. I begin by subtracting the whole numbers. 10.58 − 5 = 5.58

$$5.58 - (0.1 - 0.1 - 0.1) = 5.28$$

Next, I subtract the tenths. I can subtract 0.3 or 0.1, then 0.1, then 0.1.

$$5.28 - (0.01 - 0.01) = 5.26$$

Finally, I subtract the hundredths. I can subtract 0.02, or 0.01 and then another 0.01. I know that my difference is 5.26. 10.58 − 5.32 = 5.26

What is...?

34.45 − 3.24	89.75 − 45.42	52.48 − 10.36
9.67 − 0.51	97.84 − 24.23	44.64 − 14.33
97.35 − 34.33	94.98 − 72.26	95.96 − 84.45
79.54 − 43.16	73.77 − 12.63	95.58 − 13.27

Decomposing

What is 10.58 − 5.32?

$$10.58 \quad - \quad 5.32$$

$$(10 + 0.5 + 0.08) \quad (5 + 0.3 + 0.02)$$

I can subtract by decomposing both minuend and subtrahend.

$$10 - 5 = 5$$

I can now subtract the whole numbers, then tenths, then hundredths.

$$0.5 - 0.3 = 0.2$$

$$0.08 - 0.02 = \underline{0.06}$$

$$5.26$$

Finally, I add the partial differences to find my answer.

What is...?

2.97 − 1.22	6.75 − 2.53	9.45 − 3.23
5.67 − 2.45	8.86 − 4.52	7.79 − 3.65
13.45 − 5.24	17.78 − 12.56	29.93 − 16.81
98.76 − 46.32	124.57 − 32.34	346.99 − 212.74

Subtracting in Expanded Form

What is 29.58 – 8.36?

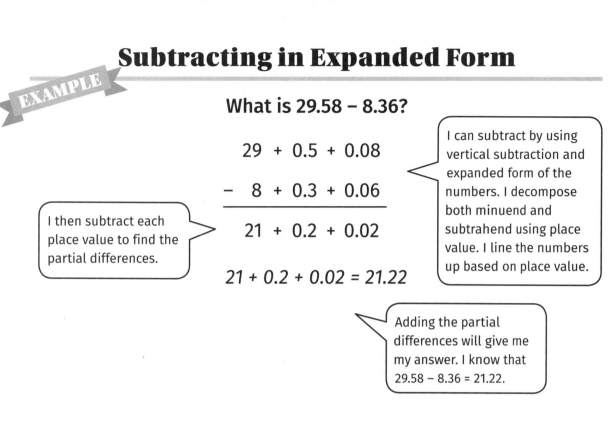

$$29 + 0.5 + 0.08$$
$$-8 + 0.3 + 0.06$$
$$\overline{21 + 0.2 + 0.02}$$

$$21 + 0.2 + 0.02 = 21.22$$

I can subtract by using vertical subtraction and expanded form of the numbers. I decompose both minuend and subtrahend using place value. I line the numbers up based on place value.

I then subtract each place value to find the partial differences.

Adding the partial differences will give me my answer. I know that 29.58 – 8.36 = 21.22.

What is...?

28.27 – 13.25	59.95 – 38.42	97.87 – 72.4
73.77 – 12.63	64.75 – 13.43	95.51 – 13.21
15.75 – 12.61	89.83 – 62.32	97.84 – 24.23
42.67 – 11.35	87.49 – 66.17	94.98 – 72.26

Decimal Strategies

Multiplying Using an Area Model

What is 0.9 × 0.7?

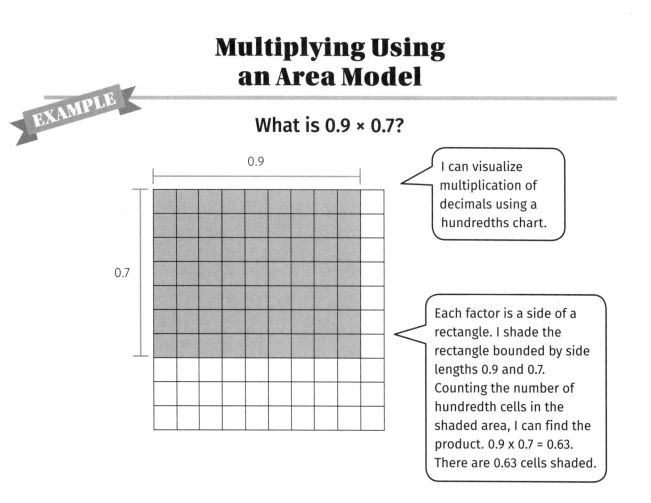

I can visualize multiplication of decimals using a hundredths chart.

Each factor is a side of a rectangle. I shade the rectangle bounded by side lengths 0.9 and 0.7. Counting the number of hundredth cells in the shaded area, I can find the product. 0.9 x 0.7 = 0.63. There are 0.63 cells shaded.

What is...?

0.5 × 0.7	0.3 × 0.9	0.8 × 0.6
0.4 × 0.7	0.7 × 0.8	0.6 × 0.6
0.9 × 0.8	0.4 × 0.9	0.6 × 0.4
0.5 × 0.9	0.6 × 0.7	0.2 × 0.8

Multiply Using an Array

What is 1.38 × 3.7?

I can use an array to multiply these numbers. I begin by decomposing both numbers based on place value and placing each as the length and width of the array.

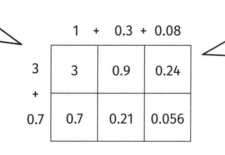

Next, I multiply 3 by 1, 0.3, and 0.08. Place the product inside each cell under the corresponding column. I will then multiply 0.7 by 1, 0.3, and 0.08, placing the product in the corresponding column.

	1 +	0.3 +	0.08
3	3	0.9	0.24
+ 0.7	0.7	0.21	0.056

3 + 0.9 + 0.24 + 0.7 + 0.21 + 0.056 = 5.106

To find the product, I find the sum of the partial products.

What is...?

2.59 × 4.1	4.49 × 7.4	9.56 × 9.1
8.27 × 9.5	6.71 × 4.3	2.47 × 1.5
9.73 × 4.2	9.98 × 4.3	8.05 × 3.7
6.38 × 9.2	5.82 × 3.4	6.45 × 3.3

Partial Products

What is 7.4 × 2.8?

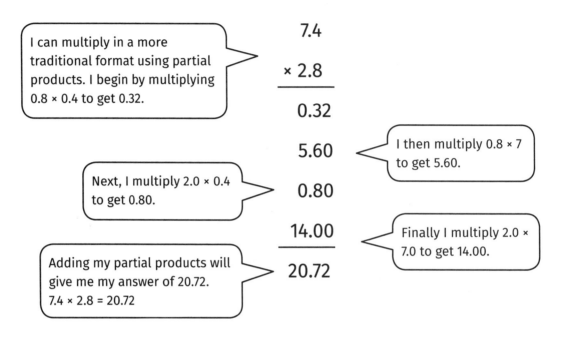

I can multiply in a more traditional format using partial products. I begin by multiplying 0.8 × 0.4 to get 0.32.

$$
\begin{array}{r}
7.4 \\
\times\ 2.8 \\
\hline
0.32 \\
5.60 \\
0.80 \\
14.00 \\
\hline
20.72
\end{array}
$$

I then multiply 0.8 × 7 to get 5.60.

Next, I multiply 2.0 × 0.4 to get 0.80.

Finally I multiply 2.0 × 7.0 to get 14.00.

Adding my partial products will give me my answer of 20.72.
7.4 × 2.8 = 20.72

What is...?

8.4 × 2.1	9.5 × 3.4	7.6 × 5.2
6.4 × 2.5	7.7 × 2.1	8.9 × 4.5
6.7 × 5.4	8.2 × 1.4	9.4 × 2.1
45.6 × 3.2	52.7 × 4.3	75.2 × 4.6

Dividing Decimals Based on Multiplication

What is 3.2 ÷ 0.4?

I begin by asking myself, "How many groups of 0.4 are in 3.2?"

I know that 8 groups of 4 is 32 or 8 x 4 = 32,

Because 8 groups of 4 is 32, I know that 8 groups of 0.4 is 3.2.

Therefore, 8 x 0.4 = 3.2.

Understanding related facts, I concluded that 3.2 ÷ 0.4 = 8.

What is...?

2.8 × 0.7	2.4 × 0.4	9.6 × 0.8
6.3 × 0.9	10.8 × 1.2	3.6 × 0.2
2.1 × 0.7	5.2 × 0.4	2.4 × 0.8
4.5 × 0.9	13.2 × 1.2	4.8 × 0.2

Integer Strategies

Adding Integers Using Tiles

What is -4 + (-2)?

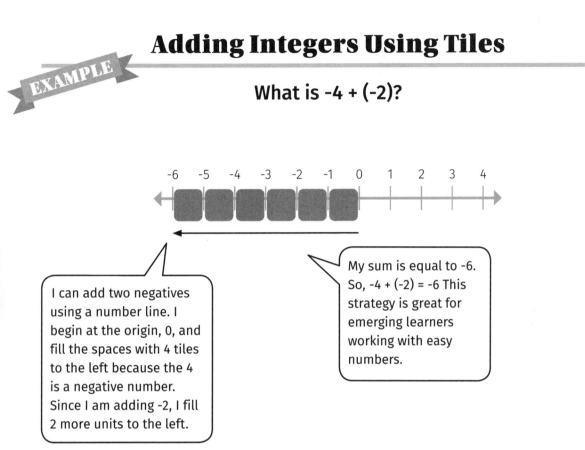

I can add two negatives using a number line. I begin at the origin, 0, and fill the spaces with 4 tiles to the left because the 4 is a negative number. Since I am adding -2, I fill 2 more units to the left.

My sum is equal to -6. So, -4 + (-2) = -6 This strategy is great for emerging learners working with easy numbers.

What is...?

-7 + (-9)	-3 + (-8)	-23 + (-3)
-10 + 4	-15 + 6	-17 + 12
24 + (-13)	13 + (-20)	42 + (-18)
-8 + (-5)	-4 + (-6)	-14 + (-9)

Adding Integers Using a Number Line

What is 3 + (-5)?

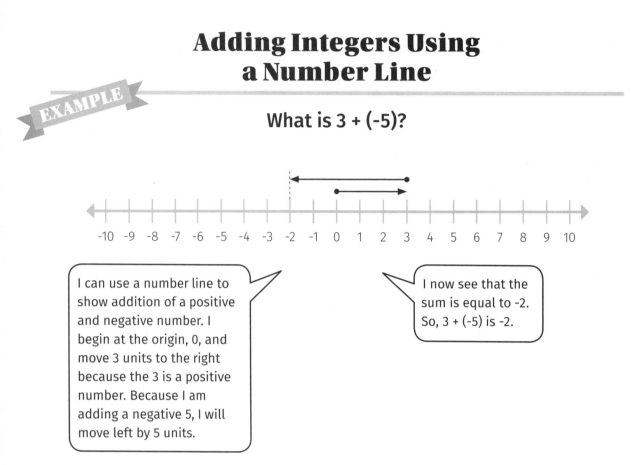

I can use a number line to show addition of a positive and negative number. I begin at the origin, 0, and move 3 units to the right because the 3 is a positive number. Because I am adding a negative 5, I will move left by 5 units.

I now see that the sum is equal to -2. So, 3 + (-5) is -2.

What is...?

8 + (-5)	-7 + (-4)	-25 + (-34)
-6 + 2	46 + (-10)	-20 + (-10)
12 + (-9)	11 + (-5)	-24 + (-6)
16 + (-8)	22 + (-6)	-14 + 22

Adding Integers Using Zero Pairs

What is -70 + 18?

Finding zero pairs will help me add quickly. I start by decomposing (-70) into the addends (-18) and (-52). I used -18 and -52 because the -18 will give me a zero pair (additive inverses) with the second addend +18.

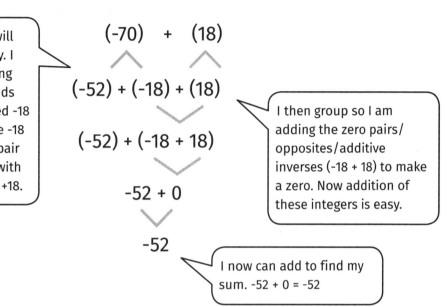

$$(-70) \quad + \quad (18)$$

$$(-52) + (-18) + (18)$$

$$(-52) + (-18 + 18)$$

$$-52 + 0$$

$$-52$$

I then group so I am adding the zero pairs/opposites/additive inverses (-18 + 18) to make a zero. Now addition of these integers is easy.

I now can add to find my sum. -52 + 0 = -52

What is...?

-20 + 14	24 + (-12)	-25 + (-34)
36 + (-39)	48 + (-60)	-20 + (-10)
-34 + (-50)	-42 + 16	-24 + (-6)
-15 + 64	22 + (-6)	-14 + 22

Adding Integers Using an Open Number Line

What is -36 + (-28)?

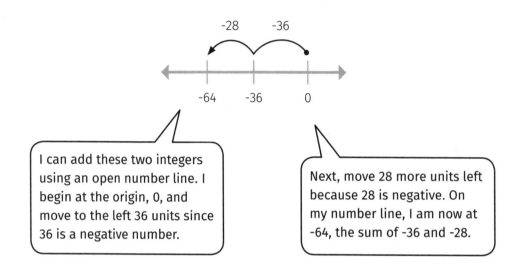

I can add these two integers using an open number line. I begin at the origin, 0, and move to the left 36 units since 36 is a negative number.

Next, move 28 more units left because 28 is negative. On my number line, I am now at -64, the sum of -36 and -28.

What is...?

-54 + 26	-49 + 35	-67 + 52
-122 + (-28)	-68 + (-32)	-37 + (-48)
98 + (-35)	63 + (-23)	88 + (-31)
45 + 65	43 + 65	56 + 39

Subtracting a Positive Integer from a Positive Integer Using a Number Line

What is 15 – 7?

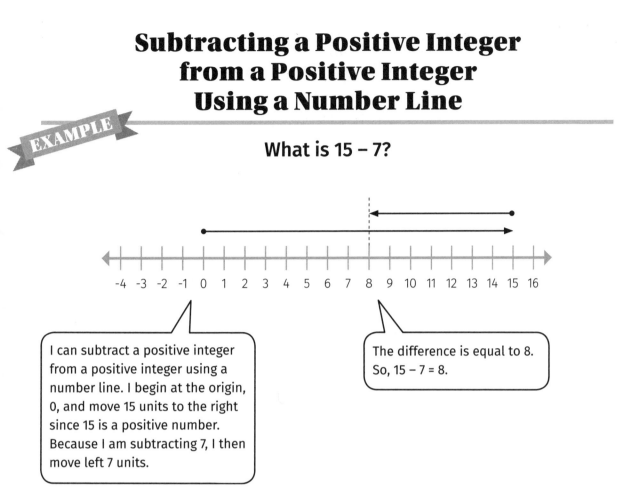

I can subtract a positive integer from a positive integer using a number line. I begin at the origin, 0, and move 15 units to the right since 15 is a positive number. Because I am subtracting 7, I then move left 7 units.

The difference is equal to 8. So, 15 – 7 = 8.

What is...?

12 – 6	17 – 6	14 – 6
9 – 4	8 – 3	7 – 5
15 – 3	14 – 9	19 – 6
22 – 13	25 – 14	28 – 17

Subtracting a Negative Integer from a Negative Integer on a Number Line

What is -12 – (-8)?

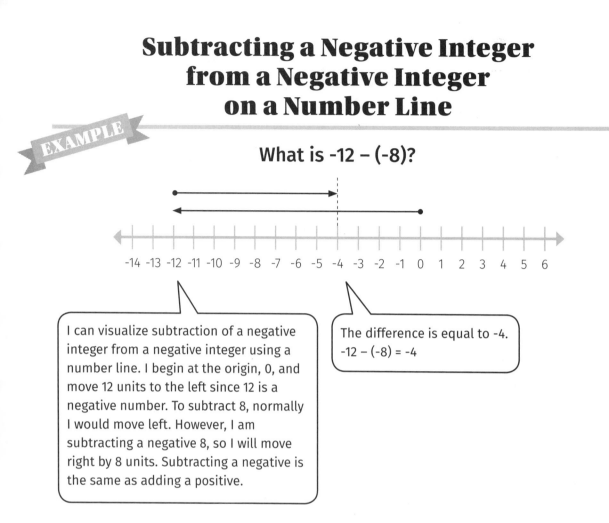

I can visualize subtraction of a negative integer from a negative integer using a number line. I begin at the origin, 0, and move 12 units to the left since 12 is a negative number. To subtract 8, normally I would move left. However, I am subtracting a negative 8, so I will move right by 8 units. Subtracting a negative is the same as adding a positive.

The difference is equal to -4.
-12 – (-8) = -4

What is...?

-15 – (-9)	-17 – (-10)	-12 – (-8)
-16 – (-5)	-23 – (-3)	-15 – (-4)
-17 – (-4)	-16 – (-9)	-19 – (-7)
-16 – (-5)	-25 – (-4)	-23 – (-5)

Subtracting a Negative Integer from a Positive Integer on a Number Line

What is 9 – (-8)?

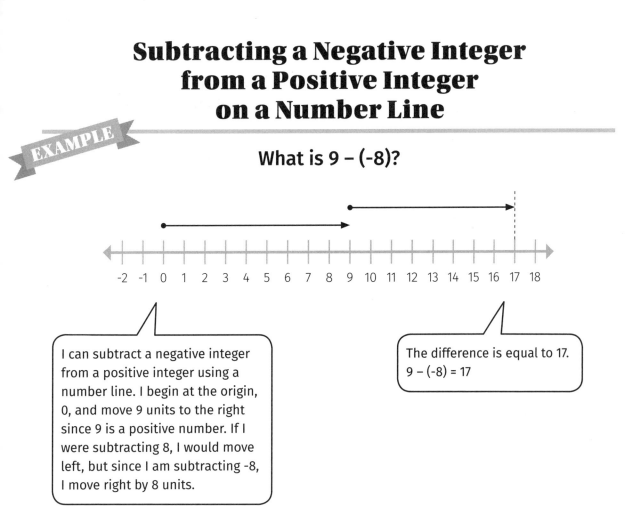

I can subtract a negative integer from a positive integer using a number line. I begin at the origin, 0, and move 9 units to the right since 9 is a positive number. If I were subtracting 8, I would move left, but since I am subtracting -8, I move right by 8 units.

The difference is equal to 17.
9 – (-8) = 17

What is...?

24 – (-6)	31 – (-3)	13 – (-8)
17 – (-9)	28 – (-5)	15 – (-3)
9 – (-9)	6 – (-12)	10 – (-10)
21 – (-7)	13 – (-21)	16 – (-4)

Subtract Negative/Positive Integers from Negative/Positive Integers on an Open Number Line

What is -120 – 72?

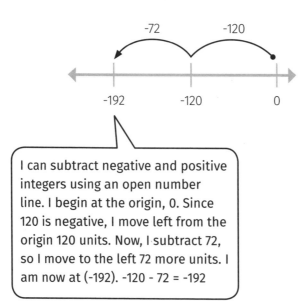

I can subtract negative and positive integers using an open number line. I begin at the origin, 0. Since 120 is negative, I move left from the origin 120 units. Now, I subtract 72, so I move to the left 72 more units. I am now at (-192). -120 - 72 = -192

What is...?

357 – 68	458 – 45	62 – (-32)
-289 – 124	-47 – 31	-64 – (-56)
-431 – 74	-154 – (-26)	28 – 29
893 – 145	-91 – 100	44 – (-81)

Subtracting Negative Integers by Finding Zero Pairs

What is 14 – (-8)?

$$(14 + 8) – (-8 + 8)$$

$$22 – 0$$

$$22$$

Just as I can add integers using zero pairs, I can do the same with subtraction. I begin by looking at the subtrahend and find its zero pair. Since the subtrahend is (-8), I add 8 to both minuend and subtrahend.

Now subtraction is easy because we have a zero pair or additive inverses. -8 + 8 = 0 and 14 + 8 is 22. 22 - 0 = 22. The distance or difference between the two numbers is 22 units.

What is...?

13 – (-5)	65 – (-34)	25 – (-14)
18 – (-23)	16 – (-11)	54 – (-43)
10 – (-26)	27 – (-15)	67 – (-56)
36 – (-29)	17 – (-31)	51 – (-51)

Subtracting Positive Integers by Finding Zero Pairs

What is -13 – 12?

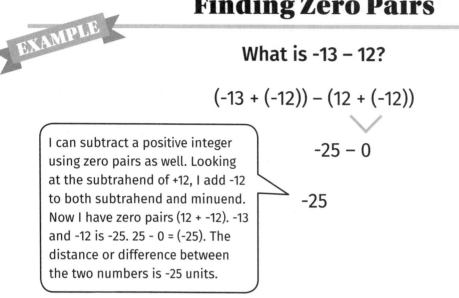

$$(-13 + (-12)) – (12 + (-12))$$

$$-25 – 0$$

$$-25$$

I can subtract a positive integer using zero pairs as well. Looking at the subtrahend of +12, I add -12 to both subtrahend and minuend. Now I have zero pairs (12 + -12). -13 and -12 is -25. 25 - 0 = (-25). The distance or difference between the two numbers is -25 units.

What is...?

-34 – 15	-56 – 45	-54 – 35
-45 – 63	-67 – 48	-21 – 21
-18 – 12	-14 – 17	-19 – 14
-36 – 25	-41 – 29	-44 – 27

Multiplying Positive Integers Using Algebra Tiles

What is 3 × 4?

Find the product of 3 and 4.

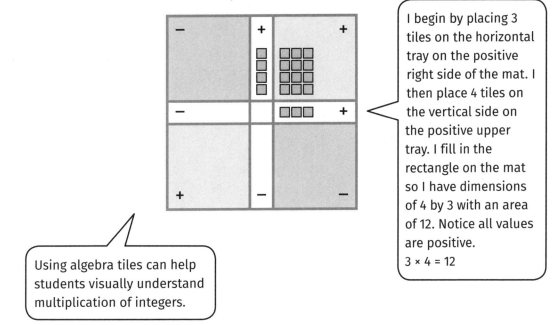

I begin by placing 3 tiles on the horizontal tray on the positive right side of the mat. I then place 4 tiles on the vertical side on the positive upper tray. I fill in the rectangle on the mat so I have dimensions of 4 by 3 with an area of 12. Notice all values are positive.

3 × 4 = 12

Using algebra tiles can help students visually understand multiplication of integers.

What is...?

5 × 6	8 × 3	9 × 12
7 × 4	4 × 5	6 × 9
2 × 12	3 × 8	9 × 5
4 × 8	5 × 6	8 × 8

Multiplying Negative/Positive Integers Using Algebra Tiles

What is -3 × 4?

Find the product of -3 and 4.

I begin by placing 3 tiles in the horizontal tray on the negative left side, since 3 is negative. I then place 4 tiles on the vertical side of the positive upper mat. I fill tiles to make a rectangle with dimensions of 4 by -3, with an area of -12. Notice the rectangle is located in the upper left side of the mat in the negative area, making the product negative. I know that -3 × 4 = -12.

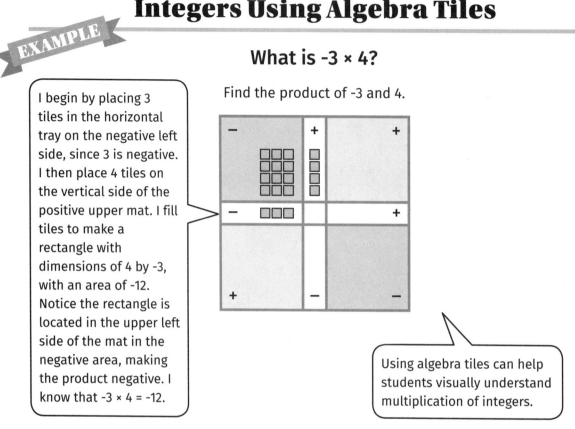

Using algebra tiles can help students visually understand multiplication of integers.

What is...?

-5 × 6	-3 × 12	-6 × 9
-7 × 7	-4 × 7	-8 × 6
-9 × 5	-10 × 4	-6 × 3
-5 × 7	-3 × 8	-9 × 4

Multiplying Positive/Negative Integers Using Algebra Tiles

What is 5 × (-2)?

Find the product of 5 and -2.

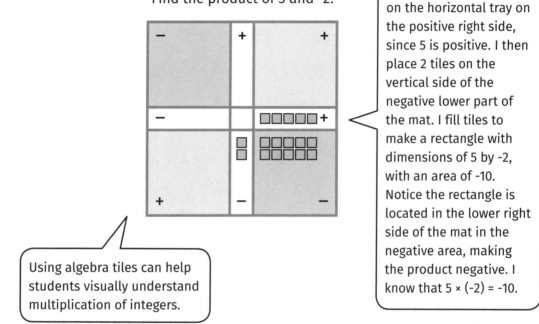

I begin by placing 5 tiles on the horizontal tray on the positive right side, since 5 is positive. I then place 2 tiles on the vertical side of the negative lower part of the mat. I fill tiles to make a rectangle with dimensions of 5 by -2, with an area of -10. Notice the rectangle is located in the lower right side of the mat in the negative area, making the product negative. I know that 5 × (-2) = -10.

Using algebra tiles can help students visually understand multiplication of integers.

What is...?

5 × (-6)	8 × (-2)	3 × (-5)
6 × (-4)	6 × (-3)	8 × (-3)
8 × (-7)	9 × (-5)	5 × (-7)
4 × (-7)	8 × (-2)	3 × (-2)

Multiplying Negative/Negative Integers Using Algebra Tiles

What is -3 × (-4)?

Find the product of -3 and -4.

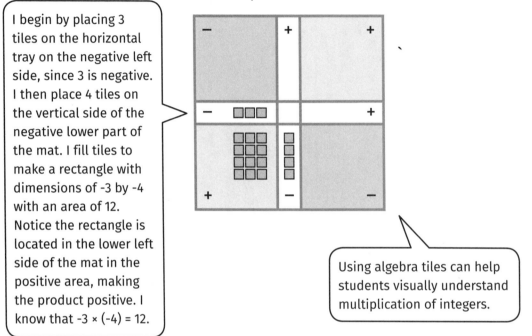

I begin by placing 3 tiles on the horizontal tray on the negative left side, since 3 is negative. I then place 4 tiles on the vertical side of the negative lower part of the mat. I fill tiles to make a rectangle with dimensions of -3 by -4 with an area of 12. Notice the rectangle is located in the lower left side of the mat in the positive area, making the product positive. I know that -3 × (-4) = 12.

Using algebra tiles can help students visually understand multiplication of integers.

What is...?

-4 × (-6)	-3 × (-9)	-6 × (-6)
-2 × (-6)	-8 × (-2)	-9 × (-4)
-4 × (-5)	-3 × (-4)	-6 × (-4)
-5 × (-3)	-2 × (-9)	-5 × (-6)

Dividing Positive Integers Using Algebra Tiles

What is the quotient of 4 and 2?

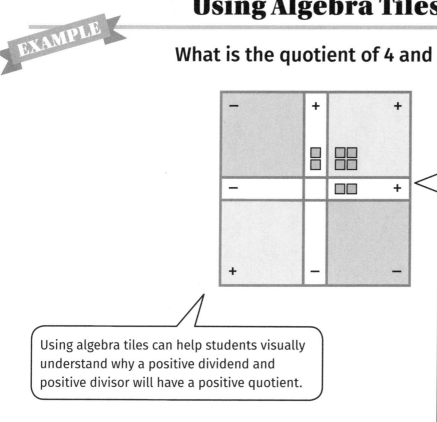

I begin by placing 4 positive tiles in the upper right side of the mat, showing a rectangular area of 4 positive square units (dividend). Since I am dividing by positive 2 (divisor), I know that one side of the rectangle will have a dimension of 2. So, I place the 2 units on the horizontal axis, positive right side. Now, it is easy to find the missing dimension. The missing side will have a dimension of 2 units. So, 4 divided by 2 will be 2.

Using algebra tiles can help students visually understand why a positive dividend and positive divisor will have a positive quotient.

What is...?

9 ÷ 3	6 ÷ 3	10 ÷ 2
1 ÷ 5	12 ÷ 4	16 ÷ 4
12 ÷ 6	24 ÷ 6	24 ÷ 4
8 ÷ 4	12 ÷ 3	18 ÷ 3

Dividing Negative/Positive Integers Using Algebra Tiles

What is the quotient of 4 and -2?

I begin by placing 4 positive tiles in the lower left side of the mat, showing a rectangular area of 4 positive square units (dividend). Since I am dividing by negative 2 (divisor), I know that one side of the rectangle will have a dimension of -2. So, I place 2 units on the vertical axis, negative left side. Now, it is easy to find the missing dimension (quotient). The missing side will have a dimension of 2 negative units. So, 4 divided by -2 will be -2.

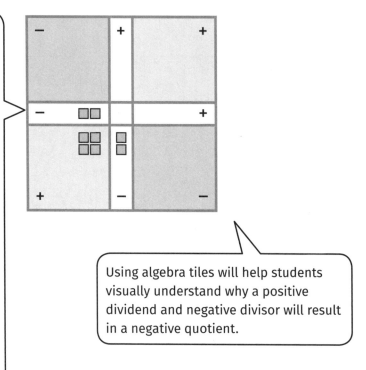

Using algebra tiles will help students visually understand why a positive dividend and negative divisor will result in a negative quotient.

What is...?

9 ÷ (-3)	6 ÷ (-3)	10 ÷ (-2)
10 ÷ (-5)	12 ÷ (-4)	16 ÷ (-4)
12 ÷ (-6)	24 ÷ (-6)	24 ÷ (-4)
8 ÷ (-4)	12 ÷ (-3)	18 ÷ (-3)

Dividing Positive/Negative Integers Using a Number Line

What is the quotient of -35 ÷ 7?

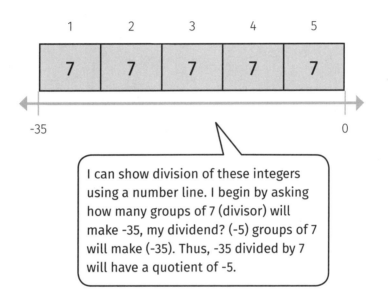

I can show division of these integers using a number line. I begin by asking how many groups of 7 (divisor) will make -35, my dividend? (-5) groups of 7 will make (-35). Thus, -35 divided by 7 will have a quotient of -5.

What is...?

-9 ÷ (-3)	6 ÷ (-3)	10 ÷ (-2)
-64 ÷ (-8)	12 ÷ (-4)	16 ÷ (-4)
-78 ÷ 6	24 ÷ (-6)	24 ÷ (-4)
16 ÷ (-4)	12 ÷ (-3)	18 ÷ (-3)

Percent Strategies

Finding Percent Using a Double Number Line

What is 40% of 500?

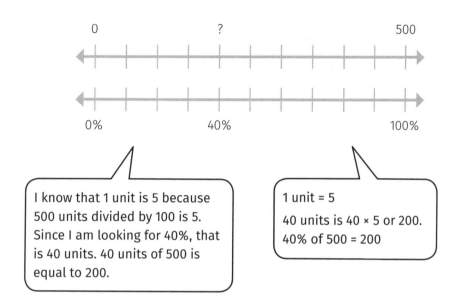

I know that 1 unit is 5 because 500 units divided by 100 is 5. Since I am looking for 40%, that is 40 units. 40 units of 500 is equal to 200.

1 unit = 5
40 units is 40 × 5 or 200.
40% of 500 = 200

What is...?

20% of 150	90% of 30	60% of 30
30% of 400	25% of 500	25% of 100
70% of 280	45% of 60	40% of 60
60% of 25	80% of 200	20% of 45

Using Friendly Percentages

What is 30% of 40?

10% of 40 = 4

20% of 40 = 8 (4 + 4)

> 30% of 40 is the same as 12 or 4 + 4 + 4.

30% of 40 = 12 (4 + 4 + 4)

40% of 40 = 16 (4 + 4 + 4 + 4)

> To find 10% of a number, I need to move the decimal point to the left one place. So, 10% of 40 is 0.1 × 40, or 4. Now it's easy to find 20% or 30%, etc.

What is...?

20% of 80	80% of 80	60% of 200
70% of 40	30% of 60	90% of 30
60% of 120	20% of 95	40% of 100
50% of 90	40% of 60	30% of 50

Tape Diagrams

What is 75% of 60?

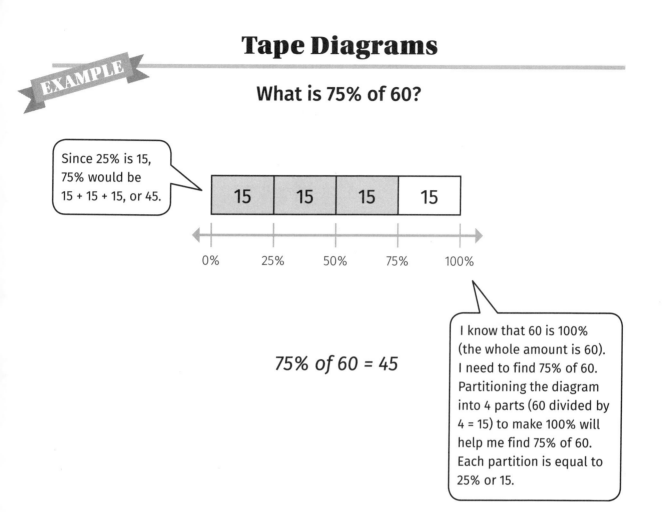

Since 25% is 15, 75% would be 15 + 15 + 15, or 45.

15   15   15   15

0%   25%   50%   75%   100%

75% of 60 = 45

I know that 60 is 100% (the whole amount is 60). I need to find 75% of 60. Partitioning the diagram into 4 parts (60 divided by 4 = 15) to make 100% will help me find 75% of 60. Each partition is equal to 25% or 15.

What is...?

20% of 80	35% of 60	40% of 80
25% of 40	60% of 200	75% of 400
80% of 100	45% of 90	20% of 75
30% of 50	25% of 180	40% of 600

Finding Percent Using a Ratio Table

What is 75% of 60?

Total	60 × .1 = 6	6 × 2.5 = 15	6 × 5 = 30	6 × 7.5 = 45	60
Percent	10%	25%	50%	75%	100%

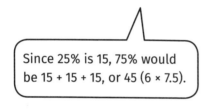

Since 25% is 15, 75% would be 15 + 15 + 15, or 45 (6 × 7.5).

I know that 60 is the whole and I am looking for the part that equals 75% of 60. I know that 100% of 60 is 60. If I know 10% of 60, it is easy to find 75% of 60. 10% of 60 is 6 (.1 × 60), 20% of 60 is 12 (6 × 2), 25% would be 6 × 2.5.

What is...?

40% of 130	40% of 20	75% of 80
20% of 40	30% of 90	70% of 140
25% of 80	20% of 210	35% of 60
80% of 120	60% of 30	20% of 100

Linear Equation Strategies

Linear Equations with One Solution—Addition

Find X.

$$x + 3 = 5$$

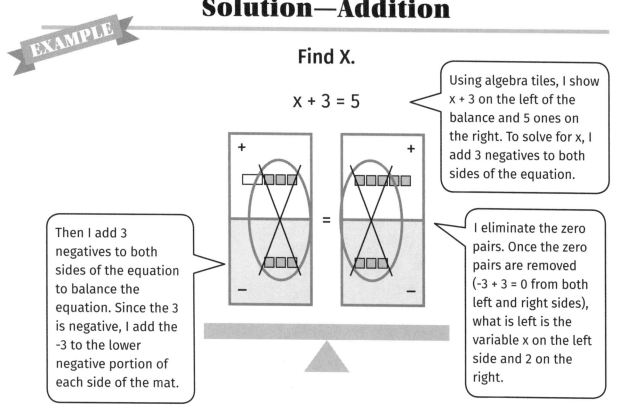

Using algebra tiles, I show x + 3 on the left of the balance and 5 ones on the right. To solve for x, I add 3 negatives to both sides of the equation.

Then I add 3 negatives to both sides of the equation to balance the equation. Since the 3 is negative, I add the -3 to the lower negative portion of each side of the mat.

I eliminate the zero pairs. Once the zero pairs are removed (-3 + 3 = 0 from both left and right sides), what is left is the variable x on the left side and 2 on the right.

What is...?

$x + 5 = (-4)$	$x + (-2) = 6$	$x + 3 = 7$
$x + 8 = (-2)$	$x + (-4) = (-9)$	$x + 7 = 10$
$x + (-6) = (-5)$	$(-3) + x = 6$	$x + 2 = 6$
$9 + x = (-2)$	$x + (-7) = 10$	$5 + x = 8$

Linear Equations with One Solution—Subtraction

EXAMPLE

Find X.

$$x - 3 = 7$$

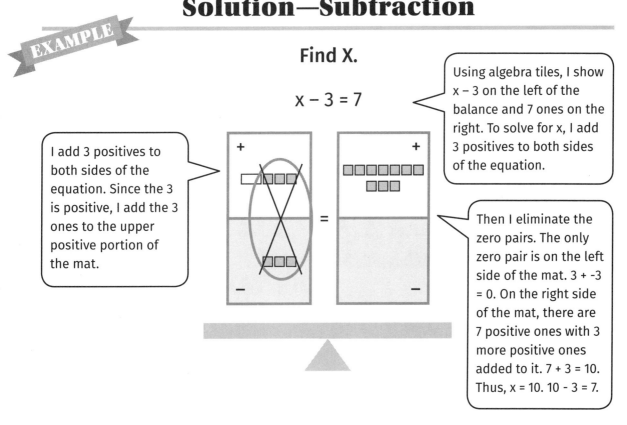

I add 3 positives to both sides of the equation. Since the 3 is positive, I add the 3 ones to the upper positive portion of the mat.

Using algebra tiles, I show x – 3 on the left of the balance and 7 ones on the right. To solve for x, I add 3 positives to both sides of the equation.

Then I eliminate the zero pairs. The only zero pair is on the left side of the mat. 3 + -3 = 0. On the right side of the mat, there are 7 positive ones with 3 more positive ones added to it. 7 + 3 = 10. Thus, x = 10. 10 - 3 = 7.

What is…?

x − 6 = (-9)	x − 4 = 7	x − 8 = (-2)
x − 4 = (-3)	x − 7 = (-1)	x − 8 = 8
x − 2 = (-7)	x − 3 = (-10)	x − 9 = (-1)
x − 2 = (-7)	x − 5 = (-8)	x − 4 = (-5)

Linear Equations with One Solution—Multiplication

Find X.

$$4x = 20$$

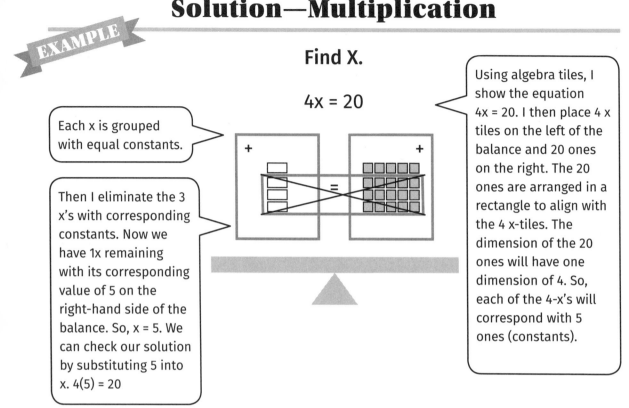

Each x is grouped with equal constants.

Then I eliminate the 3 x's with corresponding constants. Now we have 1x remaining with its corresponding value of 5 on the right-hand side of the balance. So, x = 5. We can check our solution by substituting 5 into x. 4(5) = 20

Using algebra tiles, I show the equation 4x = 20. I then place 4 x tiles on the left of the balance and 20 ones on the right. The 20 ones are arranged in a rectangle to align with the 4 x-tiles. The dimension of the 20 ones will have one dimension of 4. So, each of the 4-x's will correspond with 5 ones (constants).

What is...?

3x = 9	5x = 25	6x = 18
2x = 14	4x = 20	8x = 16
5x = 15	2x = 6	3x = 27
6x = 24	7x = 21	9x = 27

Two-Step Linear Equations with One Solution

Find X.

$$2x + 3 = 13$$

Three negatives are added to both sides of the equation.

Then I eliminate the zero pairs and group each x with equal constants.

We need to eliminate the 1x with the corresponding 5, leaving x = 5.

Using algebra tiles, I show the equation 2x + 3 = 13. Place 2 x tiles and 3 ones on the left of the balance and 13 ones on the right.

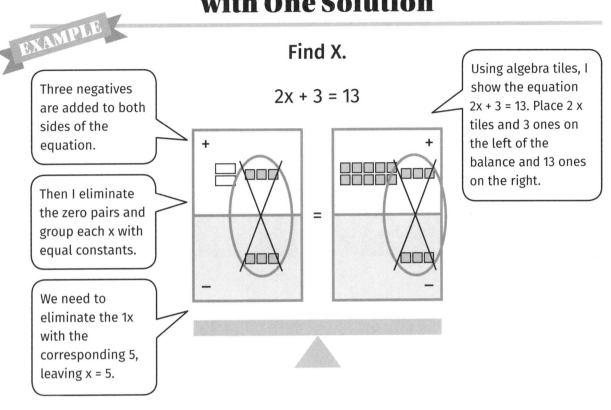

What is...?

4x + 2 = 18	2x + 5 = 23	6x − 5 = 19
3x − 7 = 8	4x − 4 = 16	5x − 3 = 22
2x − 10 = 6	3x + 6 = 12	7x − 1 = 13
5x + 2 = 12	6x + 2 = 20	7x + 4 = 17

Appendix

Classroom-Ready Number Talks for Sixth, Seventh, and Eighth Grade Teachers

Quadrant Mat

Equation Mat

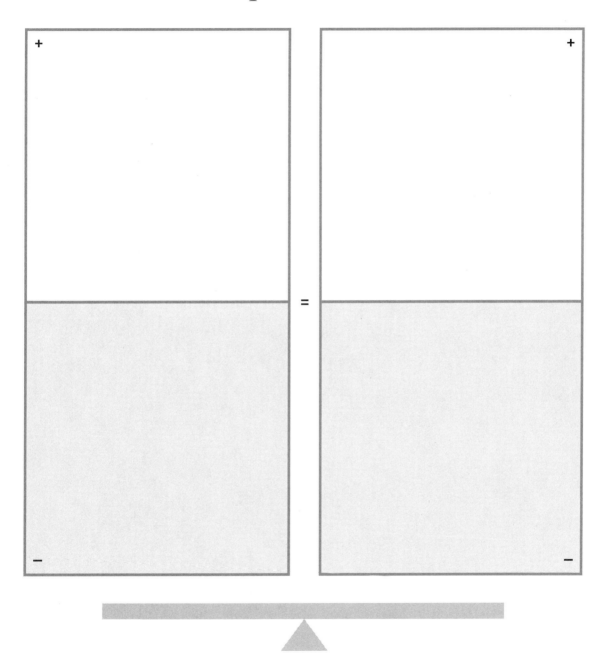

Hundredths Chart

References

McNamara, Julie, and Meghan Shaughnessy. *Beyond Pizzas & Pies: 10 Essential Strategies for Supporting Fraction Sense*. 2nd ed. Sausalito, California: Math Solutions, Houghton Mifflin Harcourt Publishing Company, 2015.

Boaler, Jo. *What's Math Got to Do With it?* New York: Viking Penguin, 2008.

Dweck, Carol. *Mindset: The New Psychology of Success*. New York: Random House, 2006.

Humphreys, Cathy, and Ruth Parker. *Making Number Talks Matter*. Portsmouth, NH: Stenhouse Publishers, 2015.

National Governors Association Center for Best Practices and Council of Chief State School Officers. *Common Core State Standards for Mathematics*. Washington, DC: National Governors Association Center for Best Practices and Council of Chief State School Officers, 2010.

University of Arizona. "Progression of Number and Operations—Fractions 2019. http://ime.math.arizona.edu/progressions/

Parrish, Sherry. *Number Talks Helping Children Build Mental Math and Computational Strategies Grades K–5*. Sausalito, California: Math Solutions, 2010.

Van de Walle, John, and Lou Ann H. Lovin. *Teaching Student Centered Mathematics: Developmentally Appropriate Instruction for Grades 5–8*. Boston, MA: Allyn and Bacon, 2006.